Gentians

Mary Bartlett

with line drawings by Rosemary Smith

Blandford Press

Contents

List of Monochrome Plates

Scale All line drawings of species bear a scale bar the full length of which represents 1 inch. The shorter division within the bar represents 1 centimetre.

List of Colour Plates

Picture Credits

Alpine Garden Society, title page, pp. 10, 121 (R. Elliott); J. Archibald, pp. 87, 143; British Museum (Natural History), p. 15; Valerie Finnis, pp. 33, 51, 90, 125; R. Fulcher, pp. 20, 69, 88–9, 108 (below); J. Horne, p. 144; R. Gibbons, p. 107; J. Parkhurst, pp. 34, 62, 149; J. S. Pringle, pp. 27, 37, 64, 70 (top left and below); J. H. Stitt, pp. 52, 126 (below); T. Underhill, pp. 108 (above), 126 (above); J. Watson, pp. 65, 70 (top right).

Foreword

The purpose of this book is to remove some of the confusion and misunderstanding which surrounds the subject and culture of gentians, and to offer a more comprehensive guide to those gardeners who find in most alpine gardening books the names of a few gentian species but who are anxious to know more about them. It strays as little as possible into the realms of alpine gardening generally as there are many admirable books on this subject.

To guide me through my early interest in gentians I relied upon David Wilkie's monograph, first published in 1936 but no longer in print. He loved and grew these plants at the Royal Botanic Garden in Edinburgh and his writing was an inspiration to me. His, and other specialists' books contained, however, very little about gentian hybrids, the American, Australasian or Japanese species, and nothing of the recent work which has been done on the genus to bring it within the International Code of Botanical Nomenclature. The nomenclature in my book has been based on *Flora Europaea*, the papers of Doctors J. S. Pringle, J. M. Gillett, H. A. Fabris, H. Toyokuni, and various other sources, thus the names used are in every case modern ones, although some of them may be unfamiliar.

In preparing my book I would like to thank the many friends and acquaintances who have given me generous assistance in the work, have undertaken photography on my behalf and kindly loaned me the results of their labours for use in this book. In particular, I would like to thank Dr J. S. Pringle of the Royal Botanical Gardens, Hamilton, Canada, who over several years has guided my search for information. I should also like to thank Mr C. Bloomfield and Mrs Y. Widger for practical help in preparing the text, Miss Rosemary Smith for undertaking all the line drawings, and lastly Tony and Leslie Birks-Hay who took so much care in producing this book.

1 A Flavour of Gentians

Some flowers have a way with them: aromatic plants inspire devotion of a sort; dahlias bring people together in droves; roses, of course, induce slavery. Gentians are amongst those flowers that can become an obsession. Not only plant collectors like Kingdon-Ward and Farrer but great Romantics like Byron and wandering spirits like D. H. Lawrence have found them fascinating and compelling, as have herbalists, artists and gardeners for centuries.

I am not sure that I want to share an obsession with D. H. Lawrence, but the hypnotic blueness of these peculiarly blue flowers touches us both, and he expresses it better than I can:

Tell me, is the gentian savage, at the top of its coarse stem?
Oh what in you can answer to this blueness?

Of course, small as they are, gentians have an advantage over more lowly plants in commanding attention, being by nature alpines. Not for them the woodland, head-hanging shyness of our native spring flowers: the small blue trumpets seem very brave, pure and clean when you come upon them on a mountainside. They bring back to me, even now as I write about them, the prickly freshness of the Alps.

As the colour plates in this book will show, gentians come in as wide a range of colours as hyacinths. When their name is borrowed by fashion designers along with aubergine, tomato, and violet, it is as absurd as calling a colour 'rose', yet everyone knows what is meant. The very word 'gentian' has an association of colour

Pl. 1 G. farreri   11

purity which makes the achievement of growing this wilful plant worthwhile.

D. H. Lawrence was no gardener, but he was more of an alpinist than I am, and he was moved by this flower. When staying in Rottach in September 1929 he wrote *Bavarian Gentians* from which these lines are extracted.

Bavarian gentians, big and dark, only dark
. . . with their blaze of darkness spread blue,
blown flat into points by the heavy white draught of the day.

D. H. Lawrence's gentian was almost certainly *Gentiana bavarica*, dark blue, but rather rare. It is only one of an enormous genus *Gentiana* comprising over 400 species, which in turn belongs to the family Gentianaceae. These best-known members of the family are very widespread across temperate and alpine regions of the world. They occur widely throughout Asia, Europe and North America, and have more than a foothold in Australasia and South America. In Asia they extend from Japan, China, Malaya, Papua, the Himalayan States, through northern India to the Caucasus; in Europe from Russia to Ireland. Farrer wrote, 'the gentians of the New World are hardly less abundant than those of the old, and on the Arctic rims of the north their fame is hardly less widespread than on the Antarctic of the south.'

Some *Gentiana* occur in Australia, and New Zealand, in its mountainous South Island, is guardian to some of the most beautiful of all white gentians, as illustrated on page 20 and page 90. In the Americas they are found from as far north as Alaska to the Magellanic tip of the southern continent. Only the Middle East and Africa have no native species.

With such a wide distribution there is immense variety of colour, habit and size. Though they are famous for their blueness, some of the most spectacular in colour are the South American species, often red-flowered. Some related genera, especially in the Himalayas, climb or trail. The largest gentian of all is the remarkable *Gentiana lutea*, yellow-flowered progenitor of the alcoholic aperitif Suze, and curer, we are told, of a multitude of ills. In the days when native species could be seen in vast numbers in the Alps, Farrer saw G. *lutea* on the slopes of Mt Cenis, flowering in August with 'a countless multitude of golden campanili'.

History

It is the curative powers of gentians, not their colour, which have the longest place in their history, and one gentian finds its way into a medicinal prescription on papyrus found between the bones of a Theban mummy.

Being so numerous and widespread, gentians have attracted to themselves the expected crop of legends and myths. King Gentius of Illyria in the Adriatic in the second century AD, who is always credited with having given his name to the family, is supposed to have known of the curative properties of the bitter, ample root of G. *lutea*; but a more romantic story is connected with Ladislaus, King of Hungary (1440–57). He prayed that if he shot an arrow in the air, the Almighty should guide it to some herb which would relieve the suffering of his plague-stricken people—and it landed on a gentian.

By the sixteenth century the wonderful plant had been introduced to England and Robert Turner records that 'it resists poisons . . . putrefaction, and the pestilence and helps digestion; the powder of the dry roots helps biting of mad dogs and venemous beasts, opens the liver and procures an appetite. Wine, wherein the herb hath been steept, being drunk, refreshes such as are over-wearied by travel or are lame in their joynts by cold or by bad lodgings.' John Gerard in the late sixteenth century indicates that it was used as an antidote for poisons. In Switzerland, according to Katherine Tynan and Frances Maitland, it was used as a cure for those who were bewitched and 'for those that had taken somewhat to fall in love with another body'. As an antidote to love *Gentiana lutea* may have had some effect. Certainly the acrid essence distilled from its root is quite a knock-out. The strong yellow drink Suze, which is popular in France and Switzerland, was originally made

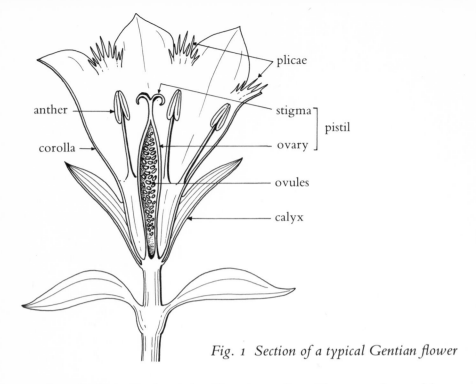

anther

corolla

plicae

stigma ⎤
        ⎥ pistil
ovary ⎦

ovules

calyx

Fig. 1 Section of a typical Gentian flower

from it, but whether it is still an ingredient I have not been able to discover from its makers. The bitter spirit of gentians has been used instead of hops in Swiss beer, and a distillation from the marsh gentian *G. pneumonanthe* was once used, as its name suggests, as a curative for lung diseases.

Apparently it was not only the love-sick and the beer drinkers who found gentians had a bitter flavour: according to Ann Pratt (*Flowering Plants and Grasses of Great Britain*) in the nineteenth century, in parts of North America where the gentian was native, 'large tracts of land with grass are left untouched by cattle', shunning the gentian much as present day herds might avoid buttercups or bracken.

Naming and taxonomy

One of the most useful things I can do for the beginner at this point, before using species names freely and without qualification,

Fig. 2 G. acaulis, as illustrated in the Botanical Magazine, *1788.*

is to try to clarify the taxonomic history of the plant, particularly in relation to *Gentiana acaulis* and gentianellas.

Tournefort (1656–1708) first used the name Gentiana in his system of classification, superseded by that of Linnaeus who in 1753 listed 23 species in *Species Plantarum*, one of them—*Gentiana acaulis*—subsequently being illustrated and described in the *Botanical Magazine* of 1788. In 1796 Froelich described 47 species, dividing them into four groups, and a major work in the classification of the family was published in 1836 by Grisebach. His preliminary work on *Gentianaceae of the World* fixed the family treatment. In 1888 Huxley, in the *Journal of the Linnean Society*, suggested a rearrangement of the genus in relation to pollen mechanism. Kusnezow in 1894 divided Linnaeus' *Gentiana* into sub-genera— *Eugentiana* and *Gentianella*—and his classification is still respected. But in 1914 no less a specialist than Farrer was calling for the abandonment of Linnaeus' *acaulis* as a name, saying it was a dead name.

Inappropriate names, like geranium, have a habit of sticking to the wrong plants, and *acaulis* is still the word used by thousands of nurserymen to describe the only gentian in their list. In this book I list and describe seven species within the *acaulis* group, any one of which may be labelled *acaulis* by nurserymen, but they are unfortunately almost equally likely to appear as 'gentianellas', for Farrer did his best to get this equally inappropriate name used instead. None of the *acaulis* types is a gentianella, taxonomically speaking. Most of the two hundred or so true *Gentianella* are of little interest to the horticulturalist: many are annuals, some are the red-flowered native species of the Andes, but one beauty from North America, *Gentianella procera*, is illustrated in colour Plate 21, page 144. Chapter 7 lists and describes some gentianellas which are correctly called by that name, but the reader must be prepared to meet the name gentianella as a synonym for *acaulis* in common or garden chat, as encouraged by Reginald Farrer who described it with affection as 'the dog who has accepted the collar of comfort and civilisation'.

Gentian hunting

Though the days of gentian hunting in the wild are gone for most of us, in certain romantic places there are still gentians to be found on inaccessible crags, and the privately sponsored botanical expedition of 1971–2 to the Andes included gentians amongst its objectives—see the Plates on pages 65 and 70.

It was the plant collectors in China, India, Burma and Tibet who, at the beginning of the present century, did much to stir people's imagination in following the fortunes of these plants. One of these was E. H. Wilson, who travelled in China on behalf of J. Veitch and Sons of Chelsea, and he was responsible for the introduction of *G. veitchiorum* from Szechwan. George Forrest, in his first Chinese expedition of 1904–7, travelled with the British Consul, Mr Litton, on the sponsorship of Messrs Bulley and Williams, who were principally interested in rhododendrons. Here he made one of his most notable finds: *G. sino-ornata* (colour

Plate 4, page 51). His only note is that he found it 'on boggy ground at a height of fourteen to fifteen thousand feet in the summit of Nie Chang Pass in the Yunnan. He made seven expeditions altogether, and died in the Yunnan in 1932.

Frank Kingdon-Ward went to this area in 1911 also under the sponsorship of A. K. Bulley, and he found and introduced *Gentiana trichotoma* and *Gentiana gilvostriata*. Not only his findings but also his writings are enlightening. He wrote of gentians in *Plant Hunting in Tibet*:

> When one remembers that every night those cups must be frozen to the consistency of parchment, and that by morning they are brittle with a thick deposit of ice-crystals my astonishment will be understood.

He noted that November and December, though cold, were the sunniest parts of the year, and that plants which can put off flowering until then are certain of ample sunlight. On the other hand they may have to ripen their seeds under snow. He also observed:

> . . . seeds were being frozen hard each night, in stiffened capsules which thawed out under the sun's rays each day. As the frost-coated capsules soften the seeds become soaked in moisture; and no sooner do they dry in the sun they are frozen again as the sun sets. This alternate wetting, drying and freezing goes on night after night.

He added that seed collected in November 1933 germinated readily in England in March and April of the following year, and his writings today may give clues on how to germinate difficult species.

Reginald Farrer, travelling with William Purdom, spent two seasons in China collecting plants, and his travels are recounted in the books *On the Eaves of the World* and *The Rainbow Bridge*. Although he had a fine eye for plants, Farrer did not collect many specimens in an area rich in material. Those he did come across might make desirable garden plants if they could be reintroduced into cultivation.

In *On the Eaves of the World* he describes seed collecting as 'the most harrowing sort of gambling as yet invented by humanity'.

> ... such are the grim and glorious uncertainties of seed collecting that, to financiers bored with the staleness of the Stock Exchange, to lovers and gamblers sickened with the monotony of their respective sports, I recommend a season of seed collecting in Tibet as a sure stimulant to their jaded capacities for excitement. ...
>
> When the blossom is over, the style protrudes farther and farther out of its mouth until about twice the length of the cup; and while the collector is vainly hunting for seed at the base of this, where the ovaries should be, and grows weary with disappointment at never finding any, lo! suddenly a little oval knob at the very tip of the style gapes open with two lips and there is the seed after all, and if you are not wary it is out and away while you watch.

His first season yielded *Gentiana hexaphylla* and, although he did not realise it at the time, it also produced his better-known introduction *Gentiana farreri*. Towards the end of his second season he found *G. farreri* in flower and wrote, 'We contemplated that marvel of luminous loveliness.' He said that, 'In addition to growing so freely and flowering so lavishly in so late and dull a moment of the year, this preposterously good-tempered exception to the rule of its race keeps its glory open, rain or shine, and layered along its shoots as complacently as any carnation.' For this plant he felt that the whole two seasons' work had been worth the effort: the problem was how to get it home, and there was no seed yet set. The live plants he transported perished on the trans-Siberian journey, but by chance some *G. farreri* seeds had been sent home in 1914 mistakenly labelled as *G. hexaphylla*. This seed was brought to flower in 1916 in the Royal Botanic Garden in Edinburgh, and named after its collector.

A gentian collector in a different part of the world was Miss A. Stafford, who collected in Peru in the 1930s. She sent home to England *Gentiana scarlatina*, which was raised and flowered at

Wisley, where it attracted a great deal of attention. The elusive South American gentians are still sought today, though they proved difficult to cultivate, even in their home continent.

Amongst other more recent gentian specialists who have made their mark are the late G. H. Berry, a keen alpine-plant gardener, who did much work in experimenting with plants and creating hybrids; and the late David Wilkie, who studied and grew gentians in Edinburgh.

Trial and Error

I first began to experiment with gentians as a horticultural student. I had seen the plants in the wild on European holidays and was keen to grow some of the more unusual species myself. I contacted botanical gardens and specialists in gentians in the hope of obtaining seed for raising plants, and was delighted to receive not only seeds, but practical advice and even plants from all over the world. I was able to persuade many American and Japanese varieties to germinate in my garden in Devon.

Of course, I tried to grow far too many species, and boxes of precious seedlings covered the garden. Cossetted as never in nature, I was prepared to protect them by covering them, even in the middle of the night, with polythene sheets against possible thunderstorms, and I even gave gentian seed frames a lion's share of the domestic fridge. I learned quite quickly that some species demand constant attention in a temperate, lowland climate. The graveyard of plant-pots with label tombstones is a discouraging sign, but a good many of the species responded and have flourished from the first.

There is no doubt, as every gardener will agree, that in a few years or so of practical experience with a plant you learn a great deal about its requirements. In regard to this nursery care, all gentians show one outstanding characteristic: they hate being disturbed. In the cultivation chapter which follows I cannot stress too strongly the need to resist the temptation to poke about in the pots and to disturb their roots.

2 Cultivation

Although he called the gentian the 'queen of the rock garden', C. E. Lucas Phillips in *The Small Garden* adds that it has a 'secret not yet discovered by the horticulturalist . . . why it will grow like a weed in one garden . . . when next door with all the care in the world it never blooms at all. . . .'

And so any chapter on cultivation must begin with both a warning—that your first efforts may be unrewarded—and a reassurance—that there are so many different types of gentians, each with different requirements, that where you *may* be lucky from the very first you certainly need not be disappointed in the end. Generalisations on the culture of gentians could be regarded as a waste of time, but I cannot resist one sweeping statement which may help the beginner to understand the nature of the plant: many gentians are flowers of the snowy parts of mountains where from the time of spring melting of the snow the roots are used to the passage of melt-water—the magic combination of wet and well-drained. Although they sound mutually exclusive, like wind and fog, these are the conditions which the amateur gardener must bear in mind when planning a gentian bed in his garden. The species which respond to other conditions will be noted later.

Siting: a general summary

In describing cultivation before propagation I must assume that the beginner has obtained his gentians from someone—and that he has one or more of the commoner species to plant in his garden.

Pl. 2 G. bellidifolia   21

The gardener who is already experienced with these flowers may find the following information useful if his results are not of the best or he wants to improve their performance.

In their mountain habitat gentians enjoy a brave burst of sunshine pretty well through their flowering season, and indeed a close grey spring or autumn in northern Europe will scarcely induce the more delicate species to open their blue trumpets. Thus in the selection of a site, adequate light is an important factor. In northerly latitudes beds should be orientated from east to west to allow for the maximum sunshine. Farther south, a north/south alignment may be just as good. Shade-loving species are noted on page 38.

Mountain environments have micro-climates of extremes, with high light intensity and rapid temperature change. As Kingdon-Ward noted, the exposed parts of plants become stiff with frost nightly, but the root systems are often protected from low temperatures by a cushion of snow. They do not experience cold damp fogs or icy rain falling on their leaves and thus frost hollows in low-lying gardens should be avoided for all gentians. However, gentians are hardy plants in the true sense of the word, and they do not need too much protection from the harsher aspects of the climate.

Though they like high light intensity, gentians do not want a great deal of heat. An open and fairly exposed position is best, away from overhanging trees. Drips from overhanging leaves irritate the gentian and deciduous leaves falling in the autumn give just the sort of mulch that most gentians least need or like. Additionally, trees make their own demands on the soil which deprive the gentians and, as will be noted elsewhere, all gentian species to a man detest root disturbance. When in competition with strong growing trees gentians will fail. It is not always, of course, practicable for the gardener to clear his land of trees for the sake of indulging his gentians, but in choosing a site one is well advised to avoid beds near trees with low overhanging branches or extensive root systems. Limes are among the worst, with honey-dew falling from the leaves in summer. Better bed-fellows are *Prunus amanogawa* and *Taxus baccata* 'Fastigiata Aurea', and for aesthetic reasons one might plant dwarf conifers near or around the gentian bed to enhance the flowers.

Trees give shelter from high winds, as often do buildings and walls. Equally, walls can create wind funnels or persistent drips as well as casting heavy shade. My own gentian garden is hemmed in by walls, which have no harmful effect whatsoever, but given the choice, my vote would be for an open situation.

In periods of prolonged rain at flowering times the flowers of plants in exposed positions can be protected from rotting and water-marking by positioning a pane of glass a few centimetres above the flowers. Four light galvanised wire supports, one at each side, will unobtrusively and safely hold the glass in place.

Soils

In their natural habitats gentians grow on a wide variety of soil types. For example, *G. verna* grows on limestone, *G. glauca* on volcanic ash in Japan, some species are found on screes and moraines, and *G. saxosa* grows on sandhills. So again, generalisations are of little use, either to the beginner or to the experienced grower. One piece of good advice for all who are trying to match plants and soil nutrients, however, is to establish the acid or alkaline balance of the soil or garden you are dealing with by means of a pH test. Small kits for measuring pH are available from horticultural suppliers, and these can be used again and again. Other kits will tell you about nitrogen, phosphate and potash content, and horticultural services are often given to gardeners for the asking. The Royal Horticultural Society will provide an analysis for a small fee, and it is worth contacting a local government department to see if information or services are available in connection with soils in your area.

If I were forced to formulate a general soil suitable for gentians, I would reluctantly suggest the substance which follows, but as species have such varied requirements I refer all readers to the species notes for more precise information.

A good friable loam free of pests and diseases is an excellent basis, with an addition of peat if you wish to lower the pH (the lower the pH number, the more acid the soil). Leaf mould should be well-composted and also checked for pH, in case it has too high a lime content. Spent hops from a brewery are a good additive, as they give an open texture to the soil. Do not use farmyard manure ever for gentians, and be wary of builders' sand, for it often contains lime or salt. Silver sand is safe, but check the source of any other sand before use in case it is likely to harm your plants.

A most important ingredient for most gentians is coarse grit or chippings, which will improve the drainage. No gentian will be happy if it is subjected to poor drainage or waterlogging. A suitable mixture for pot work is given on page 45, and other mixtures are given in L. D. Hill's *Propagation of Alpines*, pages 253–5.

Slow-release fertilisers can help gentians, providing nutrition over a long period, and some of them incorporate trace elements. Lime should not be added unless species are known to like it, and then sparingly, up to a pH of about 6. Any new bed should be allowed to settle before planting for at least three weeks, and should be kept well watered after planting.

I find an annual top dressing of half peat and half sharp sand with a little hoof and horn fertiliser will keep the bed in good condition, and this should be applied in March. Sequestered iron, containing magnesium and manganese, supplies iron in a form that stays available to the plants in the soil even in instances of high pH. It should be applied in February to March, in a wet period, once a year, the dose being half to one teaspoonful per half litre of water per plant. It is an expensive medicine and it is best to treat a trial area to see if the effects are worth large-scale application.

Colonel J. H. Stitt contends that a light soil is no good for autumn gentians. He believes that they need a heavy clay subsoil if they are to do well, as this will help to avoid drying out in summer. Plenty to drink in summer is an axiom for all species, so be ready with a watering can at all times, and never allow the soil around your gentians to go dry. If you plan to grow many different species, see if you can tap a natural source of water to provide this, the most essential of all elements for successful gentian gardening. However much it rains, there always seems to be a water shortage in a densely peopled land like England, and it is anti-social if not specifically illegal to plumb a running water supply through a rock or alpine garden. The gardener who wants to construct the next best thing must arrange for natural drainage channels to flow under the soil in which his gentians are planted, perhaps aiding them with short lengths of earthenware piping. The gardener who has the opportunity of tapping a stream or getting a natural water course to percolate under his alpine garden will find this a great asset, especially in dry seasons.

Few people have only one kind of plant in their garden, and plant associations are valuable, giving a variety of forms, shapes, textures and flowering times. Many of the ericaceous plants, Cassiopes, Daphnes, dwarf rhododendrons, and members of the Primulaceae: Cyclamen, Dodecathecons and Primulas, thrive with gentians. Bear these and their colours, together with dwarf conifers, in mind when preparing to plant your gentians.

Planting

When plants are put in during the spring they have a full season for development. Planting too late in the year often leaves the plant no chance to establish itself before the winter sets in. So spring planting is best, though it is not always practicable. Most gentians bought from nurserymen will be pot grown, allowing planting throughout the season, if required.

Before planting, the root ball should be checked to make sure it is moist. Then the plant should be carefully tapped out of the pot or removed from the wrapping, any crocks should be teased out and the plant placed firmly in position. Firming well is most essential. 'It cannot be too strongly stressed that irrespective of soil, position, or any other factor, all gentians thrive best if firmly planted.' I quote the late T.C. Mansfield, in *Alpines in Colour and Cultivation*. He goes on to say, 'Attention to this point will frequently avoid both loss of money and disappointment.'

To test for firmness, try gently pulling the plant by its crown. It should not show any sign of stirring. Take care to keep the plant watered for a few days after planting, and avoid very dry or very wet weather if possible. Check during frosty weather to see if any of the plants have been lifted by the frost. If this has happened, firm the plant back into position when the surrounding soil has thawed.

Unlike many other alpine and herbaceous plants, gentians are unlikely to become rampant and will not need keeping within bounds. Only G. *septemfida* and G. *asclepiadea* will need an annual trim and this should be when the seed has been collected and the plant has died down. The autumn-flowering species seem to prefer being tidied up in spring, although dead material should be cleaned away to deter pests and disease. Some species of doubtful hardiness can be protected with dry bracken or glass over winter.

Gentians for the border

G. *lutea* leads that group of gentians which the gardener should not hesitate to plant in the herbaceous border. The border should have a deep, well-worked friable soil, rich in nutrients. Here, G. *punctata* and some N. American species such as G. *affinis* and G. *andrewsii* will be happy, and also G. *asclepiadea* and G. *septemfida*. They will want plenty of peat or acid leaf mould worked into the soil and as a top dressing, but they will *not* want farmyard manure, however much it may suit other members of the border.

G. *asclepiadea* and G. *affinis* associate well with *Hypericum elatum* 'Elstead', *Fuchsia magellanica alba* and *Erica x mediterranea*. The strongly sculptured leaves of G. *lutea* and G. *alba*, however, are best put in bays between larger shrubs, where they can be seen in isolation.

Moving gentians

If you are forced to move your collection of plants, there are a number of ways to set about the task. We have already said that

Pl. 3 G. alba

gentians resent any root disturbance, and in the case of the larger species like G. *lutea* and G. *asclepiadea* it would be better to leave established plants and start again with young ones, as mature gentians from the herbaceous border would most probably find the move too much and die.

The time of year should be considered carefully. Spring is the best time to do the work, but if you are moving house, say, in the autumn, pot up your plants if you possibly can in the spring. They will be established in pots ready for the move and can be planted out in their new home the *next* spring.

When plants resent disturbance of their roots, this can be avoided to some extent by taking a large amount of the surrounding soil. This is appropriate to G. *verna* and G. *pyrenaica*, which will thank you for it. With G. *acaulis* and the Himalayan types, moves are not too much of a trauma (and you can take advantage of this time to divide the plants), providing the operation is not undertaken after the end of July or early August. If you are reluctant to disturb an existing garden, an alternative is to take cuttings or to try layering, and techniques are dealt with in Chapter 3 on propagation.

Any lifted plants' roots must be protected from further damage and should never be allowed to become dry. Plants can be packed firmly in trays and the roots covered with damp peat or sphagnum moss. If you need to move, take your courage in both hands and move your gentians. At least some of them will surprise you, and some of them may, with a change, grow a good deal better.

Making a gentian garden

When gentians have taken a firm hold on the gardener, he may be obliged to give over at least part of his garden to the flower and its many relations. I will try to explain how, by careful planning, this can give delight all through the year. Much as a stamp collector who specialises in one country or reign can come closer to completeness than the random collector, so a gardener with limited space can benefit by specialisation. Choosing gentians rather than, say, pinks or geraniums, will make things somewhat harder because they *are* more difficult to grow, but within a small compass one can create artificially a variety of environments of soil, shade, acidity, aspect, etc, and persuade twenty or so varieties to bloom in sequence and a wide colour range across a few square yards.

The species which hate lime, direct sun and other aspects of our environment are grouped together at the end of this chapter in the section called Positions and Conditions, but as many of the popular gentians are rock-garden subjects, the following suggestions may be helpful in creating a variety of environments appropriate to gentians within a rock garden. This is not the place to discuss the *method* of rock garden construction. I refer readers who want guidance to the standard work by B. J. B. Symons-Jeune, *Natural Rock Gardening*, and confine myself to what is of special concern to the gentian.

In landscaping a rock garden, variation in materials is almost certain to look unsightly, and in describing several I am not recommending that they should be mixed. Though local stone is more natural, you may want to build a rock garden using imported stone, and it is wise to check the acidity or alkalinity of the material you intend to use. If you are lucky enough to have a local horticultural adviser, ask for a pH test or use a pH kit as described in the section on soils. Otherwise, remember the rough and ready rule that limestone and chalk are calcium-rich and will deter species like G. *sino-ornata*.

Man-made materials can be used very effectively by enterprising gardeners. Well-worn bricks and old railway sleepers can be used for containing soil and terracing, though the gardener must plan the drainage carefully. Problems of drainage are eased if you use tufa blocks—porous light limestone which, although it releases lime, does not seem to trouble the gentians, perhaps because it also puts magnesium into the soil. Unlike other rocks, it can be tailored to shape and size with a saw, and is easily cut with a knife to make pockets for growing individual plants.* Its creamy-white colour

★ Tufa holes are only good for species with compact roots—not the tap-root type.

when bought from suppliers soon weathers to tone with local stone and soil, and it is fairly permanent, though inclined to crumble with frost. It is worth noting that the dust or waste from tufa is an excellent additive to potting composts for those gentians that like lime, such as G. *verna*.

Peat blocks are a favourite walling material in my garden, and these spade-sized pieces can be bought from garden suppliers or direct from producers in peat-cutting areas. They can be used like bricks and built in courses, bonding by overlapping the pieces, and preferably sloping back very slightly for stability, as the blocks themselves have no weight to hold back the soil. Peat, when granulated, of course, is a water-holding agent, but the blocks (which must be moistened by soaking them before any wall-building begins) are notorious for losing moisture by evaporation, and they should never be allowed to dry out. Best results are gained when the wall itself is out of the sun, and the soil behind it has an abundant source of water.

If the peat wall is to be more than 40 cm. high, some kind of support—iron rods or chestnut stakes driven vertically in front of or within the wall—will hold the structure back.

Stone and concrete troughs are good for gentians, and are much used by hybridizers who want to watch their plants at close quarters. Old glazed earthenware sinks and porous land drains are very good, as they allow surplus water to drain away, and can be filled with a carefully constituted soil to provide special conditions for any species. Land drains allow unrestricted root growth downwards and no interference from adjacent soils, though great care must be taken to set any such pipes above gravel so that drainage away is perfect.

Gentians grow well in dry walls, or in soil-filled crevices in flagged pavements, as indicated at the end of the chapter. They, especially the Himalayan varieties, thrive on scree, and this being a more specialised habitat than most amateur gardeners are likely to have to hand, it is worth describing in some detail. It is the very reverse of the rich heavy meadow-land on which G. *lutea* and G. *asclepiadea* thrive. It is unhelpful terrain, difficult to walk across in the wild, because the ice-splintered stones of which it is made are both sharp and unconsolidated. Mountain scree is not generally colonised by plants, but some love it. If the gardener wants to make a couple of square metres of simulated scree in his garden, he must choose a sloping area and dig out a good deep trench, fan-shaped in plan. At the bottom of this he must put a thickness of up to 20 cm. of coarse material, like broken flower pots, which will drain well. 'Old boots' is what Farrer recommends. A layer of upturned turf above this will prevent the topsoil from leaching downwards, and the trench should then be filled to the top with a fibrous loam/stone mixture in which the stones, such as granite chips, predominate. A top layer of chippings will allow plenty of air to circulate, which is what the gentians like.

Raised isolated beds, which help those who find bending difficult, are becoming very popular, and are well suited to gentians if the soil and drainage are right. They can be any length, but should be no higher than 80 cm. and their width should be restricted so that the centre of the bed can be reached from each side.

A garden with a rock garden, an area of scree, some isolated soil pockets, sunken land drains, a terrace with crevices and a free-standing trough or raised bed will give you plenty of opportunity for a whole host of species, and indeed, almost no excuse for failure.

Pots, pans and window boxes

For the greatest possible control of individual specimens, pots have advantages, including portability, and even the gardenless gardener can grow gentians in window boxes or in the house. Earthenware pots and pans for mature plants should be at least 15 cm. diameter and 10 cm. deep. Plastic pots need more drainage than is usually supplied but will happily split across if additional drainage holes are not carefully drilled. They should be given a good layer of crocks for perfect drainage and a soil that conforms with the requirements of the species—see the species notes in Chapter 5. A suitable general potting compost comprises two parts loam, one part peat and one part sand (with one-sixteenth grist), plus 4 oz. of John Innes base fertiliser per bushel (a bushel is equivalent to 8 gallons dry weight, that is four 2-gallon buckets or just less than two 5-litre buckets full of compost). The plant should be potted firmly in the spring, watered in and grown-on in a north-facing frame. Top dress the pots in March with 1 or 1.5 cm. of potting mixture after first removing the same depth of old compost. Once the pot becomes overcrowded it can be potted-on or divided.

Himalayan types such as *G. farreri* and *G. veitchiorum* can be given the treatment they need with pot cultivation, and so can *G. acaulis* and, surprisingly enough, *G. verna*. The great advantages of pot cultivation are that you can vary aspect, temperature, light intensity and moisture at will, though of course you need to be fairly dedicated to your plants and to have a lot of time to give to them.

Window boxes and tubs are less portable and the aspect of window boxes is determined by the house. North-facing windows do not receive enough sun and are no good for gentians. South-facing ones have too much sun and will probably dry out, so east and west aspects are best.

If non-porous containers are used, they must be at least 20 cm. deep and 15 cm. wide, or they will be difficult to keep evenly moist. As a general rule, the bigger the container, the better. Adequate holes are needed for drainage, and regular watering will be needed throughout the summer. Remember that in a window box or tub the compost will be leached of nutrients by the constant flushing of water draining through the container, and this should be corrected each spring by a top dressing of John Innes base fertiliser at the rate of 10 grams per square metre. *G. acaulis* types are suitable for window boxes, and I particularly recommend *G. lagodechiana* for tubs because of its habit. Gentians combine well in these containers with such plants as snowdrops, *Iris reticulata*, *Juniperus communis compressa*, *Genista tinctoria flore-plena*, *Jasminum parkeri* and *Rhodohypoxis*. Study your window carefully before placing the window box—according to its position it can be baking and sunny or windswept and arctic.

1 G. alpina

Gentians in the house

Gentians do not grow well as permanent house plants, but are excellent if grown in pans and brought into the house just at the point of flowering. Their striking bright blue flowers make a refreshing change from the everyday houseplant. The flowers last well in a cool room and they are protected from the weather and insect attack, which often spoil outdoor blooms. Species that do well include G. *verna*, G. *sino-ornata* and the hybrids. The spring-flowering species look attractive if the pans are made up with spring flowering bulbs so that they come into flower together.

Straight after flowering the pots and pans should be taken out again, as the plants quickly become unhealthy and yellowed: they need the clean fresh air and the abundant light that they are used to in the wild.

The dedicated gentian-grower is wounded by the thought of gentians as cut flowers, but they keep well in water, and starting with the spring-flowering G. *acaulis*, you can have gentians in the house for the greater part of the year. During the summer, G. *septemfida* and some of the large flowering types can be cut. They will last for long periods if picked immediately after bud-opening, preferably in the morning.

Those species with smallish flowers hidden by large leaves can make striking elements in floral displays if the leaves are removed up the stem, as flower arrangers do with other plants such as *Alchemilla mollis*.

In the autumn G. *sino-ornata* and the numerous hybrids are often better appreciated indoors in water as rain will spoil the corollas in the open. G. *acaulis* will often oblige with the odd flower in mid-winter, and then can be combined with miniature daffodils such as *Narcissus triandrus alba* or *Narcissus bulbocodium* as part of a floral display. G. *sino-ornata* combines with silver foliage and many of the smaller-flowering pelargoniums (geraniums), especially the ivy-leaved types.

Gentians require a warm room temperature to remain open. They do not seem to mind what other plants they are associated with in a container. G. *sino-ornata* was occasionally sold at the old Covent Garden market in London as a cut flower, and I have seen it regularly sold in bunches at local markets in the autumn. The flowers are effectively used in posies, and if a small piece of damp cotton wool is inserted into the base of the corolla it will keep them open. They can then be used as corsage flowers.

Those species which are not long-lived in water include G. *verna* and G. *pneumonanthe*.

Plants for positions and conditions

The following groupings, showing which plants to grow where, have been based on my experience in growing gentians in the south-west of England.

As many of the plants will grow in more than one type of soil condition, there is some duplication in the lists. Remember that if your plants do not succeed in the home I recommend, they may be happier in another spot.

Explanations of the recommended growing conditions are also to be found in Chapter 5, in which the species are described in detail.

Full sun with moisture
G. *acaulis* types, G. *lagodechiana*, G. *saxosa*, G. *septemfida*, G. *affinis*, G. *puberulenta*, G. *cachemirica*.

Cool and moist
This is a wet, but not waterlogged, soil, perhaps near a stream or in a valley bottom—though not on the upper banks which are often dry—lightly shaded for all or the hottest part of the day. A woodland garden of birch, *Sorbus*, *Eucalyptus* or pine, with a stream, will provide these conditions.
G. *andrewsii*, G. *asclepiadea*, G. *autumnalis*, G. *calycosa*, G. *decora*, G. *lutea*, G. *pennelliana*, G. *platypetala*, G. *pneumonanthe*, G. *rubricaulis*, G. *sceptrum*.

Pl. 4 G. rubricaulis

Open, with some shade
Many rock gardens contain a situation which is exposed to the wind from most aspects, particularly in winter, but which has shelter from the sun for part of the day by trees or shrubs.
G. alba, G. asclepiadea, G. clausa, G. glauca, G. saponaria, G. villosa.

Scree
This is an extremely well-drained soil with a large quantity of small stones or pebbles. In nature it is formed by massive accumulations of frost-broken rock at the base of cliffs and rock faces. It is not too difficult for most gardeners to create small scree habitats as part of their rock garden—see page 30.
G. acaulis types, *G. bellidifolia, G. brachyphylla, G. cachemirica, G. farreri, G. ornata, G. pumila, G. pyrenaica, G. verna.*

Moraine
A scree with a supply of running water beneath it acting as a permanent reservoir of moisture is termed a moraine. The water supply should diminish during the winter to ensure that the plant roots do not get too wet (in nature the flow is continuous). Moraines are a feature of glaciers, and are the combined result of frost action and physical crushing. Thus, the stones are very angular and irregular with large spaces between them, giving perfect drainage and copious air exchange for the roots.
G. bavarica, G. bellidifolia, G. brachyphylla, G. cachemirica, G. saxosa, G. verna.

Dry wall
Dry stone walls are used to hold back banks or raised beds of soil. Soil is used as 'mortar' and plants can be grown in this. Large stones keep the roots cool, hold a reservoir of water and, as they are raised above ground level, never become waterlogged. Watering during summer dry periods may be necessary. An isolated raised bed built by the gardener will have four aspects—north, south, east and west—extending the range of environments for different plants.
G. acaulis, G. dinarica, G. lagodechiana, G. saxosa, G. septemfida, G. verna.

Peat walls

See page 30.

G. farreri, G. hexaphylla, G. sino-ornata, G. ornata, G. veitchiorum, Himalayan hybrids.

Soil containing lime

G. angustifolia, G. bavarica, G. brachyphylla, G. clusii, G. dinarica, G. farreri, G. ligustica, G. occidentalis, G. pumila.

Lime-free soil

G. alpina, G. austromontana, G. hexaphylla, Himalayan hybrids, *G. linearis, G. ornata, G. sino-ornata, G. veitchiorum.*

Troughs

Natural stone and cast concrete troughs are commonly used to make miniature gardens for the smaller-growing species or for individual specimens. Remember that a drainage hole in the base is vital, and that an adequate depth of soil (not less than 20 cm.) is needed to prevent rapid drying out. Watering is essential during the summer.

G. acaulis types, *G. bellidifolia, G. brachyphylla, G. 'Caroli', G. farreri,* Himalayan hybrids, *G. ornata, G. saxosa, G. sino-ornata, G. pumila, G. verna.*

An alpine house

This is a cold glasshouse without any heat, used to grow alpines in pans, principally to protect them from weather damage in winter and early spring. This is for specialists and enthusiasts, who will supplement their glasshouse space with cold frames and alternate the plants between them to provide a range of interesting plants at all times in the glasshouse, where they can best be appreciated.

G. bavarica, G. bellidifolia, G. brachyphylla, Himalayan hybrids, *G. ornata, G. pumila, G. pyrenaica, G. saxosa, G. verna.*

Pockets in paving

Courtyards and patios are very popular in small gardens, especially in towns and cities. Gentians can be grown in paving and gravel in positions where they will not be walked on. Pockets of compost at least 15 cm. wide and 30 cm. deep are all that are necessary.

G. acaulis, G. x hascombensis, G. lagodechiana, G. saxosa, G. septemfida, G. sino-ornata.

Sandy soil

Such a soil contains a large proportion of inert quartz grains, from coarse to very fine in size. The degree of drainage and aeration of such soils naturally depends on the size of the grains, but they are free from the danger of waterlogging. These soils need good watering in the summer to satisfy gentians.

G. dinarica, G. lagodechiana, G. saxosa, G. septemfida, G. pumila, G. verna.

Heavy, but not waterlogged, soil

G. acaulis, G. asclepiadea, G. lagodechiana, G. lutea, G. pneumon-anthe, G. septemfida.

The herbaceous border

G. affinis, G. alba, G. andrewsii, G. asclepiadea, G. lutea, G. punctata, G. septemfida.

Pots

G. acaulis, G. farreri, G. x hascombensis, G. saxosa, G. veitchiorum, G. verna, Himalayan hybrids.

Window boxes and tubs

G. acaulis, G. dinarica, G. x hascombensis, G. lagodechiana, G. septemfida, G. sino-ornata.

Seaside

Gardens by the sea provide one of the most hostile environments for gentians. The drying winds, salt desiccation and growth distortion due to prevailing shore winds preclude practically all species. G. saxosa from New Zealand and G. verna from western

Ireland are amongst the species which grow naturally by the sea, but they grow in conjunction with other plants and gain some protection from the climate. Protection by means of screens, hedges and fences will help. The following species are worth trying, to see if they will tolerate your own particular seaside garden conditions.

G. *acaulis*, G. *dinarica*, G. *glauca*, G. *lagodechiana*, G. *saxosa*, G. *septemfida*.

East or north positions, with a little morning sun

G. *acaulis*, G. *asclepiadea*, G. *clusii*, G. *dinarica*, G. *lagodechiana*, G. *septemfida*.

Species suitable for cutting for flower arrangements

G. *acaulis* types, G. *farreri*, Himalayan hybrids, G. *lagodechiana*, G. *septemfida*, G. *sino-ornata*.

Species for beginners

G. *angustifolia*, G. *dinarica*, G. *lagodechiana*, G. *saxosa*, G. *septemfida*, G. *sino-ornata*.

Fig. 3 **a**: *flower ready for pollination, showing pistil surrounded by anthers.* **b**: *section showing pollen being removed from ripe anthers.* **c**: *section showing anthers removed and stigma ready for cross-pollination or hybridisation.* **d**: *pollen from anthers being placed on to the stigma to fertilise the ovules in the ovary.* **e**: *seed pod swelling showing the seed is ripening.* **f**: *seed falling from ripe pod, to be caught in a porous, labelled packet.*

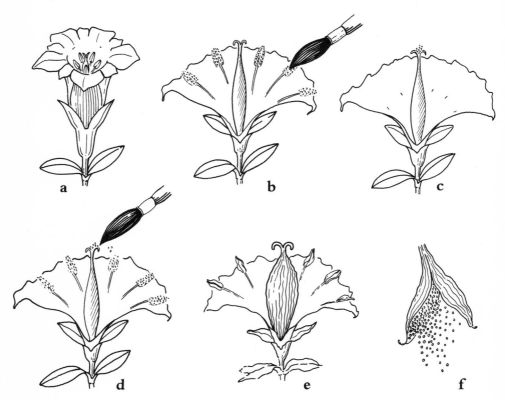

3 Propagation

It is best, for the beginner, to start with some good healthy plants from the nurseryman, choosing robust plants of an easy species. Results will come quicker from established plants; propagation takes time. Be encouraged, however, that gentians can be propagated by seed, cuttings, division and by layering. Certain methods are more appropriate to certain species, according to their habit— those with a central rosette for example are not handily divided, and instructions where appropriate are given in the species notes.

Seed

Nearly all gentians set an abundant amount of seed, often with hundreds in each capsule. Gentian seed can be obtained from seedsmen, or through the numerous seed exchanges around the world, or by means of the advertising columns in the *Quarterly Bulletin of the Alpine Garden Society*, but for those who want to propagate from the seed of their own plants the following notes may be useful. Species such as *G. acaulis*, *G. verna*, *G. septemfida* and *G. lagodechiana* are perfectly happy pollinating themselves. But with some of the Himalayan species such as *G. ornata*, *G. hexaphylla*, *G. veitchiorum* and *G. farreri* a little help from the gardener is appreciated. Hand pollination is easily carried out using a camel-hair paintbrush. Depending upon the weather, the flower opens showing the anthers clustered around the pistil. As the flower matures the anthers part, showing the pistil in the centre. When the anthers are full of pollen the stigma has begun to reflex.

This is the time to pollinate and it is best done on a fine sunny day. Using the brush gently, place the pollen from the anthers on the stigma. The pistil will swell and split when the seeds are ripe, in about two to three weeks. It is advisable after fertilisation when the seed pod begins to swell to tear the corolla to stop moisture being retained at the base of the ripening seed pod. The seed is ripe when the ends of the pod begin to curl and the pod becomes brown in colour.

Collect the ripe seed carefully and make sure if you are going to store it that it is correctly labelled with all relevant details, including the date. Keep it in porous packets.

Many gentian seeds, especially those of high alpine species, are best planted at once as they would be in nature, for gentian seed quickly loses its freshness or viability, and old seed takes a very long time—years—to germinate. The only problem with the immediate planting of fresh seed is the difficulty of establishing the young seedlings in the winter. With New Zealand species imported into the northern hemisphere there is no problem, as freshly gathered seed from New Zealand can be planted in the northern spring.

As a general rule for sowing seed, Wilkie says, 'see that the seed is fresh, the best method being to sow as soon as the seed is harvested . . . whenever possible the seed should not be kept until the spring but sown at once.'

For amateur gardeners, without special propagation facilities, I think it is important that there should be long enough left in the growing season for the seedlings to become established. Thus, I believe that seed collected later than August should be kept until the New Year. Do not put it away in a drawer or damp greenhouse, but give it the conditions which will best protect its viability. If you can, keep it in an airtight container with some silica gel to reduce humidity, and make sure it is cool by keeping, if convenient, in a refrigerator. You will thus suspend animation.

As gentian seeds are so small there is a danger of sowing too thickly, giving rise to weak, overcrowded seedlings. Fine seed can be well mixed with fine dry sand before sowing to avoid the crush.

It is important to get the soil mixture right. It should be light and porous, with perfect drainage. A mixture of sterilised loam, sharp sand and peat in equal parts is recommended. Take care that it contains no lime, especially for the lime-hating species such as G. *sino-ornata*. Make sure that pots and seed pans are perfectly clean (see Chapter 4) and use a piece of perforated zinc at the bottom of seed pans to keep out worms without impairing drainage. A layer of crocks or grit can be placed on top of the zinc, below the soil mixture. The compost mixture should be lightly firmed by hand and the seeds sown thinly, then covered with fine compost. Alternatively the seeds can be sown on top of a thin layer of fine silver sand, and left uncovered.

An alternative method for G. *verna* is to scatter fresh seed directly on to the soil in a trough. Do not cover this seed at all. Good germination should occur the following spring and the plants will flower twelve months later.

There seems to be an irresistible urge when sprinkling seed to use everything that is in the packet, and not to waste any. It is better to prepare too many pots and pans than to risk overcrowding in this way. Over-wintered seed should be sown in January or February.

Top-sown seed must be watered from above only with a fine spray, so that the seeds are not washed about, but watering both pots and seed pans from the bottom is much to be preferred. They can be sunk out of doors up to the rim in sand and covered with glass so that moisture from the surrounding sand is drawn through the compost and the surface is protected from the rain. They should be kept in the shade and allowed to germinate. In the winter pots can be freely exposed to frost and snow—if they are made of plastic they will not crack.

For the results of research on germination readers are referred to Prof. F. E. Weiss (*R.H.S. Journal*, Vol. 58, page 296), who discounts the need for mycorrhizal fungus, and to P. A. Thompson (*Journal Hort. Sci.* 1969, Vol. 44, pages 343–58). Thompson's work indicates the varying conditions required for different sections of the genus. For instance, the section Aptera is shown to germinate

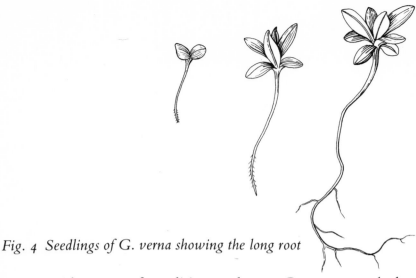

Fig. 4 Seedlings of G. verna showing the long root

over a wide range of conditions, whereas G. *pneumonanthe* has specific temperature requirements for germination and responds to chilling. However, in section Coelanthe no species germinated without preliminary chilling treatment. A common requirement for all species is light during germination and the optimum chilling temperature is thought to be 2° Centigrade for a period of between four and twelve weeks. Extended research carried out by G. H. Berry on G. *verna* is detailed in *Gentians in the Garden*, pages 33–7. He concludes that G. *verna* seeds will germinate always in March, no matter when they are sown, except that seed planted after January will remain dormant until March of the following year.

If you have the patience to keep sown but inactive seed pans for several years you may ultimately be surprised by the appearance of seedlings, though the results are likely to be rather patchy.

Seedlings begin to grow rapidly if put into a frame or taken into the greenhouse. Allow them plenty of air but no direct sunlight. Often if seed pans are retained for a further year after pricking off more seedlings will appear so do not discard the seed pans when you have removed the first crop of seedlings. Once the seedlings are big enough to handle, with some true leaves, they should be carefully pricked off in to pans or boxes. The seedlings resent root disturbance and care should be taken in handling them as the smallest of seeds produce a long length of root. Such species as G. *verna* are better pricked off in clumps of three to four. A light, well-drained soil should be used for potting on, allowing plenty of room for the seedlings to develop. Those which are not large enough to be pricked out before the end of June are best left until the following season.

Advantage should be taken of the many types of pots, compost, boxes and even waste plastic food containers such as yoghurt pots now so embarrassingly available. Compressed peat pots 3 cm. square will allow the pricked out seedlings to become well established individually without the roots being ripped apart at transplanting time as happens if they are pricked out into larger boxes. However, care must be taken when these compressed peat pots are placed in soil that the peat is completely submerged, or that its top is broken off to soil level. If it is at all exposed it will act as a wick, robbing the young plant of essential moisture.

Newly pricked out seedlings should be kept cool until they have recovered from the shock to their system, and should be given plenty of air but protected from the sun. The roots should never be allowed to dry out. When thoroughly established, the young plants are best planted out in springtime, allowing them a growing season to become settled in their permanent home.

Cuttings

Every gardener likes to try his hand with cuttings. Taking cuttings is a quick and useful form of propagation but is not suited to all species of gentians and some species respond with only moderate vigour. Though an attractive way of increasing your stock, it is not as reliable as propagation from seed or by division. Cuttings from the Himalayan species such as G. *farreri*, G. *hexaphylla*, G. *veitchiorum* and G. *sino-ornata* are most likely to give good results, although the G. *acaulis* group will also take root, and likewise species that send up a series of shoots from the base such as G. *septemfida* and G. *lagodechiana*. Taking cuttings is not possible with the species which have a central rosette and long tap root.

The best season for taking cuttings is spring as later cuttings are unlikely to produce enough root to see themselves happily through the winter and into the next season, when they can be planted out.

A suitable shoot for cutting will be 4–6 cm. long and will be fairly close to the crown of the plant. Pulling the cutting from the parent plant will have the usual wounding effect on the tissue and will leave the gentian in some disarray, so a sharp knife is essential and the cut should be made below a leaf joint. Strip off some of the lower leaves, and if you believe in hormone rooting powders dip the cleaned end into a powder recommended for soft-wood cuttings. Give the stem a gentle tap to shake off any surplus powder. With some species the cuttings seem to have an adverse reaction to hormone rooting powder, and rot rather than root. Those rooting powders which contain Captan are preferable to others as they provide protection against pathogenic fungi.

More important than chemical stimulus is quick action. All cuttings are casualties and must be given first aid; to leave them lying around in sun or, worse still, in the pocket is often fatal and they must be planted immediately to avoid wilting. When collecting, keep them in a polythene bag.

Most of the shoots made from cuttings are destined by nature to produce a flower bud, probably at their tip. Opinions vary as to whether this should be picked off so that the cutting may use its energy in producing roots. My experience, however, is that the flowering may not be detrimental provided that any flowers produced are removed when they are over so that they do not rot.

Cuttings should be placed 2–2.5 cm. apart in a well-drained compost of peat, sand and ground pumice or vermiculite. If placed too close together the cuttings will rot or the roots will become intertwined and potting up will become more difficult than is necessary. The cuttings should be set vertically, well firmed and watered and kept shaded from direct sunlight. Cuttings of the Himalayan types root from the callus and upper nodes. Commercial growers have had considerable success by using mist propagation for gentian cuttings, though for modest numbers such a procedure is unnecessary. I have used mist propagation with gentians but the cuttings rooted in this way need careful handling as with the slightest provocation the roots will fail or even fall off because of high humidity.

After potting, the cuttings should be well watered in and left undisturbed in the rooting medium for at least four to six weeks to get a decent root system established. Rooting will be assisted by keeping the cuttings indoors and humid under a sheet of glass or in a polythene tent. If cuttings are potted individually rather than in trays there will be less disturbance to the roots when they are moved and the root ball can be transferred intact. Rooted cuttings should be potted on the fresh compost and put in a shaded frame or cool greenhouse through the summer. They may be planted into permanent positions in the open either in the autumn to harden off in time for winter, or in spring according to their vigour.

Do not, if you can help it, use weak or sickly plants as stock for cuttings. Cuttings taken from young material will always grow more quickly than from old. Certain cherished plants, if they show signs of disease or old age, can be persuaded to pass on their good qualities to a new generation of cuttings, but if you have any doubts about the health of the parent plant, isolate and watch the cuttings carefully in case they inherit disease.

Vegetative propagation is the only way of maintaining the colour or special characteristics of named cultivars and hybrids which cannot be trusted to come true from seed, and fortunately many of the hybrid gentians have an appropriate habit for cuttings —details of propagation methods are given in Chapter 6.

The disappointment of seeing an army of cuttings weakening and giving up the struggle can often be avoided if you do not subject them all to the same soil and conditions. Spread them around and keep them at different temperatures if you have the room and the time. Try, too, a variety of containers for rooting cuttings—there are so many now available, of varying shapes and sizes, made of polythene, plastic, clay or peat. My own experience is that the plastic containers are the best for even growth. Clay pots lose moisture unevenly and the cuttings do not like this.

Division

It may seem sacrilege to split up for division a healthy mat of G. *acaulis* into the risky limbo of smaller incomplete plants, but propagation by division suits some species well and you will see results from your new stock much more quickly than if you start from seed.

I believe that dividing Himalayan types every third year contributes to their well-being and ensures that you do not have in your garden ageing gentians—like ageing dogs, lovable but an awful sight.

The ideal plant for division is one that forms a dense mat with many fibrous roots. It is no use trying to propagate the central-rosette tap-root varieties this way. Gentians of the *acaulis* group and G. *sino-ornata* are particularly happily divided. Early spring, before growth recommences, is the best time for division though it is not the only time. Some species will divide well after flowering and G. *acaulis* types can be divided in June. Division too late in the season will not allow the young plant to make a satisfactory root system before the autumn and the winter will perhaps be worse than such a plant can bear. Ideally, division should be completed no later than July.

Lift the whole clump and pull it gently apart, taking care to disturb the roots as little as possible. The mat will usually fall into six or seven sections, not necessarily all the same size, and these should be separated by cutting with a knife if necessary. Teasing the mat to pieces will be more harmful to a sensitive plant than a clean cut.

G. *sino-ornata* seems to invite division by exposing many small shoots each with a root system when the clump is lifted, and these separate easily and grow well. Other species to try are G. *veitchiorum*, G. *farreri* and G. *ornata*. Do not attempt to divide G. *verna*: its roots are far too sensitive for this operation and you are better off to grow it from seed.

Divided plants can be replanted with fresh compost either in pots (and then kept in a cold frame until they are established) or

3 (above) G. makinoi; 4 (below) G. sino-ornata

direct into their permanent quarters in the garden, thus avoiding a second root disturbance and a second check. If you want an intermediate stage in pots try peat or fibre pots which can be broken away, allowing the plant and all the soil to be placed in the earth when strong enough.

As with seedlings and cuttings, care must be taken that the divided plants do not dry out during the six to ten weeks after planting, so keep your new stock well watered.

Layering

This form of propagation is well suited to Himalayan types and hybrids. Layering will often occur naturally as the stem lies close to the ground. Expert opinions differ on whether it is the flowering stem which produces roots or the side shoots producing roots near their junction with this flowering stem. The result of such rooting is what matters: a small new rosette of leaves left when the flowering stem has dried off. Layering can be induced by pegging down shoots in the spring or using small pebbles to keep the shoots in close contact with the soil below, as shown in Fig. 5, below.

Layered plants are best left until the season following their initial rooting, and only cut from the mother plant in the following spring when they will be transferred into fresh compost in pots

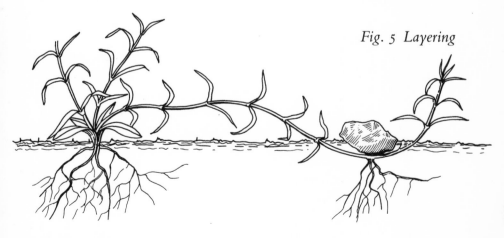

Fig. 5 Layering

◀ 5 G. acaulis

for a season in the nursery. The species best suited to layering are *G. hexaphylla*, *G. farreri*, *G. 'Macaulayi'* and *G.* 'Kidbrooke Seedling'.

Give some layered plants, cuttings or seedlings to your friends, and do not be ashamed to ask for some of the resulting plants back, if theirs have taken and yours have not. Always be ready to increase and replenish your stock: gentians only have a certain life span and young plants are always needed to replace them.

Collecting plants

With the growing awareness all over the world of the need to conserve native flora, collecting the whole plant is a practice frowned upon in most countries. With up to date methods of propagation it should no longer be necessary. In many countries, including Switzerland, there are lists of plants protected by law, and these should be respected for the benefit of everyone. Species fully protected by the proposed British Wildlife Protection Bill include *G. verna*.

A wild plant collector's licence is necessary in some countries, including Britain, and anyone planning to collect wild plants when abroad should enquire of their own Customs if special permission is necessary. There are no restrictions on the importation of seed, but plant health certificates issued by the exporting country must accompany plants, other than those collected in the wild, when importation is made.

Observing these regulations saves such embarrassment as having a hidden bundle confiscated by the Customs, and prevents the importing of unwanted pests and disease. Gone are the days when whole pieces of sod were dug up and transported, and some careful thought should be given to any project involving the collection of wild, unprotected, species, as many are unlikely to survive a long journey. *G. acaulis* plants transplant well, but species with long tap roots suffer such a check that they rarely recover. Rare specimens must, of course, be left intact. Collect seed if you can, but preferably only from a plant which you have seen in flower: this will prevent the disappointment of raising an inferior, unwanted plant.

Flowering times vary as you climb higher in the mountains. In early spring flowers will only be found in the lower pastures. As the snow recedes plants will flower higher and higher up the mountainside, and by this time the lower plants may have set seed. Altitude can also affect the size of the plant and the flower. At high altitudes plants are often compact and neat because of the high light intensity and hard growing conditions, and some experienced collectors believe these plants taken high up will be hardier than those from lower down.

It is wise to heel any specimens collected into a temporary garden until the day before returning home, when they can be washed clean of any soil, the roots wrapped with damp moss or paper tissues, put into polythene bags and packed tightly to prevent jolting. On arrival, the bags should be opened immediately to prevent rotting, and the plants dealt with as soon as possible. If travelling for a longish period it is best to use a stout container filled with suitable compost, moist peat or sphagnum moss. Keep such a box away from the sun or it will act as an oven and bake your plants to death. If you embark on any kind of collection always label specimens and seeds carefully with notes about local soil conditions as well as date and, if relevant, altitude. A photograph taken at the time of collection can be a great help in identifying seeds later.

The subject of plant collection is dealt with in greater depth in a very readable article by A. Huxley, 'The ethics of plant hunting', published in *The Journal of the Royal Horticultural Society*, June 1974.

4 Pests and diseases

I put up a strong resistance to reading about plant pests and diseases until they actually happen, and then I regret it. The damping off of cuttings or seedlings or the discolouration of leaves and the failure of flower buds is so depressing that protection is well worth while. No gardener can hope to keep all his plants healthy all the time, but it helps if he knows the enemy. Thus, a wide range of possible troublemakers are described below, not all of which are associated with the gentian family. Luckily gentians are not particularly disease or pest prone. If we satisfy the considerable demands they make for soil, drainage and aspect they are likely to stay healthy and perform to the gardener's delight. If they become sick the following may be responsible.

Pests

Ants Ants can be a problem to gentians, especially in light sandy soils. They eat seeds and sap the plant's energy by encouraging greenfly. They are most active in the late spring and early summer when the nests are expanding. Ant's nests are not difficult to find, since the scurrying insects are always pointing the way. They should be destroyed by dusting with BHC (benzene hexachloride), a standby chemical for all gardeners, repeating after ten days if necessary. An alternative method is to pour boiling water on the colony but this is only recommended if the nest is well away from the roots of plants. *Nippon*, an organic ant killer, is good and safe: the method is to put three or four drops on a piece of wood or glass near the ants' runs, repeating every three or four days until there is no further sign of activity. Rain destroys the effectiveness of this poison, therefore you should cover the product or repeat the dose after wet spells.

Aphids Everyone knows the greenfly, almost omnivorous where plants are concerned, and certainly not averse to feeding off gentians. In addition to distorting growth and impairing flowering, they can transmist viruses. Symptoms of attack include mottling, distortion or puckering of leaves, stickiness of foliage owing to honey-dew, ants feeding on the honey-dew and loss of vigour in the plants.

Try to reduce the aphid population by using organic pesticides such as Derris and Pyrethrum. The systemic materials are very good, especially those supplied in aerosol form, and if used according to the instructions the aerosol canisters can be as economical as other sprays.

Cutworms This is the name given to the tiresome caterpillars of certain moths in the *Noctuidae* family. They feed on the plant around ground level, frequently severing stems from tap roots. They can be controlled by a combined BHC and DDT dust.

Leatherjackets These are the grubs or larvae of daddy-longlegs or crane-flies, and are usually more common in damp weather during the summer, as the newly hatched grubs cannot withstand drought. Attacking the underground stems of the plant, they can easily be overlooked in the soil, owing to their earthy colour. They have natural predators, such as viruses, parasites and birds, and they can be chemically controlled with BHC, should a serious infestation occur.

Red Spider In a hot, dry summer, this pest can be found attacking a wide range of host plants. Visible signs of attack are mottling of the leaves and webs covering small areas of the leaf, but this damage can occur at any time from April onwards. The webs can expand rapidly in warm, dry conditions, sometimes encasing the plant stem as well. This pest has become resistant to many poisons. Fortunately it has several natural predators and recent research work has made control by predators the safest and easiest method. The small round mite *Phytoseiulus persimilis* is a predator which can be introduced to the affected plants in May before the build-up of a large population of red spider mites. Some measure of control can also be effected by damping down the foliage, as the mites are deterred by cold, damp conditions.

Seed-eating Caterpillars Seed pods are occasionally attacked by a variety of insects seeking the nutritious seed. When hybridising or saving gentian seed, a wise precaution is to dust or spray the pod with BHC every ten days.

Slugs and Snails The slug is not an attractive creature. Together with snails it can be a major pest on rock gardens, feeding throughout the year. The irregular damage to leaves and buds, and the characteristic slime trails, are indications of their presence, but night time, with a torch, is when you see the culprits at their work. Slugs are eaten by birds, frogs, hedgehogs and moles, and of course the song thrush actively seeks out snails.

Metaldehyde baits are cheap and effective and can be bought ready-prepared or made up in pellets. Spread them evenly around your gentians: they have a habit of coming out of the packet in a rush and you should try to arrange that they make an even ring around the plants, so that slugs are distracted on their way to the plant. If preparing one's own bait allow 20 grams of Metaldehyde to every kilo of bait, e.g. stale breadcrumbs.

A newer material is Methiocarb which is better in wetter conditions and has the added advantage of killing leatherjackets.

Thrips These are tiny insects which, during warm summer weather, cause considerable spotting and flecking marks on leaves and blooms, spoiling their appearance, distorting growth and causing dying shoots. As soon as symptoms are noted, a protective spray of BHC should be applied. Give a second application two or three weeks later for good measure.

58

Weevils These insects often attack plants in pots, when their grubs damage the root system below soil level, and often this is not noticed until the plant has suffered severely. I have been troubled with the vine weevil larva, a creature about 6–8 mm long, easily recognised by its creamy white body and tan or yellow-coloured head. Control can be by drenching the pots with BHC at the rate of 10 centilitres of 20 per cent gamma BHC concentrate to 22 litres of water. Unfortunately this does not always penetrate under the crown on the plant. Five per cent DDT dust can be incorporated in the potting compost at a rate of 200 grams per bushel when potting stock plants if a recurrence of attack is likely. One expert recommends removing the plant from the pot, washing the soil from the roots, and re-potting in fresh soil, making sure that all grubs are destroyed.

Woodlice These insects are very destructive, feeding on decaying matter and seedlings or soft stemmed plants. They congregate in rubbish at the bottom of pots, under loosefitting stones, or beneath carpeting plants such as Phlox. Rock gardeners are always turning them up under their rocks. They can be controlled by trapping in upturned flowerpots with hay or woodwool. Chemical control is with BHC dusted around the hiding places frequented by the woodlice.

Worms Gardeners have reason to thank worms, for all the soil turning that they do. But gentian roots, as a rule, hate disturbance, and worms in plant pots change the structure of the soil and compost and upset the drainage by blocking up the drainage holes as well as disturbing the roots of the plants. Watering with Derris or potassium permanganate solution should eliminate worm activity. Then water the foliage with clean water to avoid staining.

Diseases

Not much research has been done on gentian diseases, since the economic importance of the plant is slight. However, there are certain rusts and fungi which are particularly troublesome to gentians, and some complaints that gentians are as likely to catch as are other plants.

Rust   Rust fungi are one of the most difficult groups of pathogens to deal with, as they are extremely resistant to chemical measures. *Puccinia gentianae* attacks some members of the genus causing light and dark brown pustules on the leaves. Severe attacks can result in the death of the plant. Control is by picking off affected leaves and burning them. Severely attacked plants should be dug up and burned. Never re-plant gentians in soil that is known to have suffered from this fungus. Rusts are specific fungi and therefore this species of rust will devote itself entirely to your gentians. On the other hand, rusts such as *P. menthae* on garden mint will not attack.

Stem Rot   Gentians are susceptible to a range of root and stem rots where soil drainage and moisture reserves are inadequate. Himalayan types are particularly at risk. A light dusting of the plant's roots with Zineb or Captan can give some protection at planting time. Spraying with freshly-mixed Bordeaux compound at fortnightly intervals will help to control the spread of disease. Bordeaux mixture can be made in a plastic bucket as follows: 100 grams of copper sulphate, 125 grams of hydrated lime, to 10 litres of water. It should be used when freshly mixed.

Damping off   An all-too-common occurrence in boxes and pans of seedlings. The causative fungi, *Pythium de baryanum* and *Rhizoctonia solani* are encouraged by moist conditions, as found in over-watered, poorly drained and overcrowded seedlings. The spores for the initial attack are commonly found in unsterilised soil, dirty boxes and pans, so the answer lies in cleanliness. Boxes, pots and pans should be washed or sterilized, either by steam or with formalin, and the latter can be bought as a concentrate for using in a 2 per cent solution (i.e. 1 litre per 49 litres of water). The equipment and tools should be stacked, watered well and then covered with tarpaulin, polythene or sacking to hold in the formalin vapours. After twenty-four hours the covers can be removed and the vapours allowed to disperse, this taking about three days. Any loam used for propagating must be sterilised. Such loam can be purchased and treated with formalin at the rate of 10 litres per square metre of loam, stacked 20 cm. deep. Up to five such layers may be safely built and treated at one time. The whole stack should be covered for forty-eight hours. Up to three weeks should elapse before using the loam; if the loam is turned weekly this will assist in clearing the vapour. Steam sterilisation is an easier method—quicker—but expensive, and best left for large-scale operators. An alternative method for controlling *P. de baryanum* is to water the box of seedlings or cuttings with Cheshunt compound (two parts copper sulphate, eleven parts ammonium carbonate, applied at the rate of 30 grams per 5 litres). Although useful this is not as effective as sterilisation, and does not control *Rhizoctonia* species, weed seeds or soil-borne pests.

Botrytis   This is a grey mould which appears particularly on later-flowering plants, coating foliage and discolouring petals. It can be a problem in poorly-ventilated alpine houses and frames. The leaves and flowers quickly turn soft under the masses of woolly fungal growth. Infected material should be picked off and burnt. Spraying or dusting with Zineb will give protection. An airy, dry atmosphere, however, is the best safeguard.

Virus Diseases   Little is known of gentian viruses. It is quite possible, however, that there are injurious or deleterious viruses specific to gentians, as well as those with a wide host range occurring in many different genera. When bringing new plants into an existing collection, always ensure that they are healthy and buy them from a reputable nurseryman. Seed propagation greatly lessens the risk of virus spread, as few viruses are known to be transmitted by seed.

Visual symptoms are not a ready guide. If a plant is mottled or off-colour it may be a virus or it may be due to cultural or nutritional failings.

Pl. 5 G. acaulis, white form,
photographed in the wild.

5 The Species

It must be difficult for a gentian of the dwarf, stemless variety to manage to feel a family relationship with some of its tall herbaceous cousins. With over four hundred true gentians within the genus Gentiana, distributed in nature as widely as indicated in Chapter 1, there are differences of appearance which would readily confound a beginner. A specialist in gentians will recognise the Great Danes and the Pekingese amongst the breed but, as with many dog lovers, they keep a special affection for a small group with certain characteristics in common. It would take exceptional devotion to love every single one the same.

E. B. Anderson, late President of the Alpine Garden Society, said of the Gentianaceae, 'A very large family which contains more plants with wonderful blue flowers than any other. It also contains some coarse and ugly ones.' I very much agree with him, and in this long chapter devoted to descriptions of the species, I have deliberately included only those which are beautiful, or special, or specially beautiful, plus a few interesting mavericks. I have kept annuals quite separate—see Chapter 8—together with the South American and New Guinean species, which are fascinating but so remote from garden cultivation that they are best kept on their own. The next chapter deals with hybrids, and the most important *Gentianellas* are described in Chapter 7.

In the Table on pages 150–3 some 120 or so true species (but not annuals, sub-species, related genera or hybrids) are listed with their vital statistics and cultural requirements. Those who seek even more species are referred to the Royal Horticultural Society

Pl. 6 G. hooperi, from Mexico

Dictionary, which describes nearly 200 species and hybrids, and David Wilkie's monograph listing several hundred.

All the gentians I describe have their country of origin included but, of course, the majority can be cultivated anywhere, and are in cultivation wherever gardens flourish. It may be helpful, nevertheless, to group them according to their native geography.

European gentians Mainly spring flowering, dark 'gentian blue' in colour and usually evergreen, the European group includes the big names: *acaulis*, *verna* and *lutea*. And, of course, Europe includes the Alps and other appropriate mountain habitats from Iberia to the Balkans.

Himalayan gentians These include the paler blue gentians which flower in the Autumn: the jewels brought back by the great plant-hunters at the beginning of this century such as Wilson (*G. veitchiorum*), Forrest (*G. sino-ornata*) and Farrer (*G. hexaphylla* and *G. farreri*). Himalayan gentians are often striped and marked with green. Although many are slow to increase, they are easy to propagate, and have been parents to more of the popular hybrids (such as G. *'Bernardii'* and G. *'Inverleith'*) than any other group. They are all thirsty in Summer and need very good drainage. Many of them are

64

Pl. 7 G. sandiensis, Peru

difficult to distinguish from one another when they are not in flower and they need careful labelling.

With Himalayan gentians may be grouped other Asiatic species such as the Japanese species, with which they are botanically allied.

North American gentians Summer and Autumn flowering and very varied in type and habitat, native North American gentians include those in which the corolla remains closed or nearly closed as with the 'closed gentians' G. *andrewsii* (colour Plate 9, page 70) and G. *rubricaulis* (Plate 4, page 37). Many are of an unusual colour and they are generally easy to grow if seed is available in seedsmen's lists.

There are more cultivated gentianellas (see Chapter 7) in North America than elsewhere and these include the beautiful annual fringed gentian, *Gentianella procera* (colour Plate 21, page 144).

South American gentians Tremendously numerous and varied, South American gentians account for a large proportion of the members of the genus. Many have bright flowers, notably red and yellow, and often the flower is cup- or crocus-shaped, but they have scarcely been brought into

65

cultivation even in South America. This continent also contains many gentianellas.

New Zealand gentians The Southern Alps are the home of a number of gentians with a strong family resemblance. They are often white with darker markings and have no plicae. They include *G. bellidifolia* (Plate 2, page 20), *G. corymbifera* and *G. serotina*.

Even in New Zealand difficulty has been found in growing these natives as garden plants and many of them produce few seeds. *G. saxosa* (colour Plate 13, page 90), however, is famous throughout the world.

The Species

The Acaulis Group

'The big trumpets' (G. H. Berry)

It is difficult to know what exactly was the original plant named and described by Linnaeus in 1753, and I intend to treat *acaulis* as a related group of species and sub-species, following Professor T. G. Tutin's paper on the section *Megalanthe*. He distinguishes several *acaulis* types and states:

> The morphological differences between the taxa are slight, the best characters being provided by leaf-shape, the relative lengths of the tube and teeth of the calyx, and the shape of the calyx-teeth themselves. On the other hand they are clearly separated ecologically or geographically. *G. acaulis* and *G. alpina* are calcifuge, while the remainder are calcicole. The greater number of taxa in the calcicole group is perhaps a reflection of the disjunct occurrence of calcareous rocks.

The seven types have many features in common, and their physical variations are given at the end of this section.

G. acaulis is the name you will find listed in your seedsman's catalogue and this could be one of the several similar species

66

commonly known as bell-gentian, or misleadingly as *Gentianella*. In some gardens it will bloom prolifically with little attention; in others it refuses to flower. That is the secret of its success. Give a gardener a perennial puzzle and he will be contented. Contented, that is, to wrestle with it year after year and to compare his results with his neighbour's and his diary of past years, like the owner of a vineyard. There is no doubt that some gentians are more amenable and willing in the garden than are the *acaulis* types, but I am reluctant to say that any is more rewarding, for the greatest reward of all to the gentian-lover is to be favoured not with a predictable burst of blossom but with an unexpected perfect bloom. Of the many gentians that bestow their favours irregularly, the *acaulis* types are the most magical, for in the deep bells of their flowers lies the true gentian blue.

When you have succeeded with *Gentiana acaulis* you will love gentians always. If you have not succeeded every writer on the subject will have some advice for you, often conflicting. Wilkie recounts some of the more bizarre rituals: 'beating the soil as hard as possible before planting;.tearing the plant to bits every second year.' My own advice is as follows; plant in a moist and well-drained position in the full sun. With a considerable amount of peat added to the compost, my plants flower well each year and there is often an odd bloom out of season, even in mid-Winter. I conscientiously avoid lime, but a colleague has excellent results on a limey soil. This sort of counter-point perhaps gives us a clue. Similar species developing naturally on different soils develop different requirements; what you have bought as *acaulis* may not be the same stock as your neighbour's. But if it is and you still fail where he succeeds, try planting somewhere else in your garden. Ideally, give as many different plants as many different sites and treatments as you can manage.

G. *acaulis* certainly seems to be affected by micro-climates, but the long-held theory that some kind of fungus in the soil is necessary as a 'catalyst' has long since been disproved by F. E. Weiss.★

★ F. E. Weiss, R.H.S. Journal, Vol. 58, p. 296.

Gentiana acaulis L. (The Alps, North-east Spain, Central Italy, Central Yugoslavia)   *Col. plate 5, p. 52*

Syn. *G. excisa, G. kochiana*
Variable in height between five and ten centimetres, with lanceolate, elliptical or infrequently obovate deep-green glossy leaves at the basal rosette. The deep-blue bell-shaped flowers are produced during May or June. The calyx teeth are usually less than half as long as the tube, ovate and strongly narrowed at the base. The calyx corolla has green spots on the inside with deeper blue markings at the throat. It is usually lime-hating although it is found on acid rocks in limestone areas. 'Acaulis' means stemless, though not all the flowers appear without a stalk. *G. acaulis* is the chosen symbol of the Alpine Garden Society, the epitome of the rock garden.

Gentiana alpina Vill. (Alps, Pyrenees, Spain) *Col. plate 1, p. 33*

Usually only attaining a height of seven to eight centimetres, this dwarf species is a rare plant in its native habitats. The rosette leaves are leathery in texture, dull green in colour and sub-orbicular in shape. The deep blue flowers with darker markings and green spots on the throat, are produced singly, often without a stem, in July. The calyx teeth are about half as long as the tube and the corolla lobes are obtuse. It is distinguished from *G. acaulis* by the funnel shape of its corolla.

It is a little more difficult to grow than some of its relations. It is said to be a lime-hater and Chopinet recommends a sandy soil (one-third peat, one-third compost and one-third sand).

Gentiana angustifolia Vill. (South West Alps, Jura)   *Fig. 8*

In this species the rosette leaves are dull green in colour and linear-lanceolate to oblanceolate in shape—longer and thinner than other *acaulis* types. Reaching a height of about ten centimetres, the slender flowering stems usually have one or two pairs of leaves

6 G. *lagodechiana*

and larger flowers than those of the G. *acaulis*. Blooms are produced in July and are funnel or bell-shaped, sky-blue (rather lighter than other *acaulis* types) with a pale inside and green spots in the throat. The calyx lobes stand out from the tube and are usually less than half as long as the tube, lanceolate and narrowed at the base.

This is one of the best species of the group and does well in cultivation. It likes an open well-drained position. Although found in the wild in limestone areas it does not appear to need lime in the garden.

Gentiana clusii Perr. et Song (Central and eastern Alps) *Fig. 6*

This, as can be seen from the Figure which shows *acaulis* types drawn to the same scale, is one of the largest flowered species. The rosette leaves are elliptical to oblong-lanceolate, bright green in colour, stiff and leathery in texture. The flowers are deep azure blue, paler in the throat with fewer green spots or none at all. The corolla is funnel or bell-shaped, and the calyx-teeth are usually at least half as long as the tube, triangular and widest at the base. G. *clusii* flowers in June and in nature is found growing in limestone areas. In cultivation, therefore, it likes lime in the soil.

There are two sub-species: *clusii*, which has the margins of the leaves strongly papillose (warty) and sub-species *costei*, with weakly papillose leaf margins.

Gentiana dinarica G. Beck (S.W. Yugoslavia, Albania) *Page 1*

This is a species with a small distribution. The plant reaches a height of up to 7 cm., and the leaves in the rosette are bright green and broadly elliptical in shape. The bright blue funnel or bell-shaped flowers are produced during June and have no green spots in the throat. The calyx-teeth are about half as long as the tube, narrowly lanceolate and narrowed at the base. G. *dinarica* is free flowering in cultivation and is one of the easiest of the group to grow. Like G. *clusii* it is found in calcareous soils and likes lime.

7 (top left) G. linearis; 8 (top right) G. incurva;   71
9 (below) G. andrewsii

Gentiana ligustica Vilmorin et Chopinet (Maritime Alps, central Apennines) *Fig. 7*

This species has rosette leaves, oblong in shape or oblong-obovate to broadly ovate, up to three times as long as they are wide. The blue flowers, produced in June and July, have greenish spots in the throat. The calyx teeth are less than half as long as the tube, broadly ovate and narrowed at the base. This is another member of the group which occurs naturally in limestone areas.

Gentiana occidentalis Jakowatz (Western Pyrenees, Cordillera, Cantabrica)
This is a localised species rarely seen in cultivation. The base or rosette leaves are elliptical to oblong-lanceolate. The beautiful deep blue flowers are produced in June and are unspotted in the throat. The calyx teeth are usually more than half as long as the tube, ovate to lanceolate, narrowed at the base. This is another species which grows in limestone areas. Chopinet suggests that G. *occidentalis* may be intermediate between G. *clusii* and G. *angustifolia*.

The Acaulis Group—Summary

The family likeness of the *acaulis* types is undeniable, although there are many minor variations and plants often do not fit into any of the basic descriptions above. The extent of hybridisation in the wild is unknown and experimental work in the field is necessary. Additional names which are used to describe members of the *acaulis* group are G. *grandiflora*, *latifolia* and *vulgaris*, but these are no longer regarded as taxonomically correct. In nursery catalogues other variations are given such names as 'Coelestina', 'Maxima' and Alba. A white *acaulis* photographed in the wild at 1,800 metres is illustrated in Plate 5, page 62.

Gentiana affinis Griseb. (N. America) *Fig. 9*

This gentian is widely distributed in North America from Saskatchewan, Manitoba and North Dakota to British Columbia

Fig. 6 G. *clusii*

Fig. 7 G. *ligustica*

Fig. 8 G. *angustifolia*

73

Fig. 9 G. affinis

and south to Nevada and Arizona. It is an erect species producing
shoots reaching about 30 cm. in height from stout branched
yellow tap roots. The leaves are obovate to oblong. The funnel-
shaped flowers are borne in cymes, often in threes, sometimes
more, in August/September and they can vary in colour from
green to deep blue. G. H. Berry, growing *G. affinis* in England,
found the flower stems fragile and in need of support, though it is

said to be a good plant for a herbaceous border. Several writers go out of their way to state that it is an 'attractive plant', though without any real enthusiasm.

Growing in sedge meadows in the wild, G. *affinis* is found in close association with *Potentilla fruticosa*. It likes a light, well-drained, lime free soil, full sun and adequate moisture, and grows on meadow land, in valleys and foothills to quite far up the mountainside. The plant shows considerable variation according to its altitude, the number of flowers per stem, and the size of calyx lobes. It is often grouped with other species such as *G. forwoodii*, native to Wyoming, *G. bigelovii*, native to Arizona and *G. interrupta*, native to Colorado. Dr Gillett suggests that all should be treated as a single species.

Gentiana alba Muhl. (N. America)   *Plate 3, p. 27*

Another North American species native to the prairies in the middle states of America and Canada, its extent is defined by Dr J. S. Pringle as southern Michigan to central Minnesota, south to Kentucky, north-western Arkansas and eastern Kansas, with scattered populations east to southern Ontario, eastern Pennsylvania, west Virginia and western North Carolina. It is a robust plant with a coarse spreading habit reaching a height of up to 60 cm. Leaves lanceolate to ovate. Flowering August/September, the bell shaped flowers are produced in large dense clusters, white with prominent green veins, and only opening at the top of the corolla.

It is often found in association with the big Blue-stem Grass (*Andropogon gerardii*) and other prairie species. In cultivation a good deep soil with ample moisture seems to be the most successful.

It is not a popular species and little grown horticulturally, as many people regard it as ugly. Some, however, find it valuable for its vigour and prolific flowering, and it would be a species worth trying to hybridize, in order to raise a form more attractive to horticulture.

75

Gentiana algida Pallas (N. America, Asia)   *Fig. 10*

Syn. *G. romanzovii*
This is a species with a wide distribution across the roof of the
world from Siberia and Japan to Alaska and North America in
general. Dr Gillett gives its North American range as Pribilof
Island in the Bering Sea, the Aleutian Chain, coastal and interior
Alaska, the western Yukon and with considerable disjunction
down to Montana, Wyoming and Colorado.

Reaching a height of 5–20 cm. its stems are angled and yellow-
green in colour, with leaves linear to linear-lanceolate in shape.
The flowers appearing during August and September are often
borne singly, yellow or whitish-green, with purple or blue-green
spots on the corolla, which is funnel-shaped.

It is best propagated by seed and cultivated on a well-drained
soil. Its Latin name means 'cold, of high mountains' and it is closely
related to *G. frigida*. Its common name in Japan is Toyaku-rindo,
or 'whitish gentian' (the suffix 'rindo' is Japanese for gentian).
There is a Japanese form *G. igarashii*, with a common name
Kumio-rindo or Yezo-rindo, which has larger, more beautiful
flowers and grows on high wind-swept places in central Honshu.

Gentiana andrewsii Griseb. (N. America)   *Col. plate 9, p. 70*

This rugged plant, named after H. C. Andrews, the English
botanist, is a native of north-eastern America and Canada, where
it is predominantly a prairie species.

Several leafy stems are produced from a central root stock and
these reach over 30 cm. in height, with dark green lanceolate to
ovate leaves in pairs up the stems. The flowers are club-shaped and
are borne in the axils of the leaf and in clusters at the top of the
stems. Flowering is from mid-August to early October, and the
blue, or occasionally white, flowers remain tightly closed, which
gives rise to the common name 'closed gentian'. Dr Pringle
divides the species into two varieties: *andrewsii* and var. *dakotica*,
the difference between the two being that *dakotica* has slightly

Fig. 10 G. algida

larger corolla lobes, and its distribution is slightly to the west of var. *andrewsii*.

This gentian is easily cultivated in ordinary soil with some peat added, and it prefers slight shade. It is best propagated by seed. Although the flower remains closed it is an attractive species more suited to the border than the rock garden and it makes an excellent display in summer.

Gentiana asclepiadea L. (Europe, Asia Minor) *Fig.* 11

This species comes from central and southern Europe and extends into Asia Minor and the Caucasus.

Commonly known as the 'willow gentian' this is one of the large species suitable for the herbaceous border or the woodland garden. It has a graceful arching habit, the slender stems having heart-shaped leaves in pairs. The narrowly bell-shaped flowers stand erect on the stem, often in pairs, sometimes more, and they are produced from July to September. They are rich blue, spotted inside with purple, and with purple stripes on the outside of the bell. *G. asclepiadea* grows well in damp shady places in the wild, and likes a cool, moist soil. According to Farrer it is lime-tolerant. It can be increased by seed, careful division or from pre-flowering thick-stemmed cuttings taken in May or June. The flowering shoots need to be trimmed annually after seeds have been collected.

There are a number of forms and flower colours, all varying in flowering time and height. Commonly grown is the white variety *G. asclepiadea alba*, which makes a slightly smaller plant. It can be planted in association with many plants, such as *Polygonum vaccinifolium*.

Gentiana austromontana Pringle et Sharp (N. America)

Growing at high elevations in western North America, from Southern Virginia to north-eastern Tennessee and western Carolina, this plant reaches 30–45 cm. in height and has glossy green ovate to lanceolate leaves. It is perhaps the most beautiful of the 'closed' or 'bottle' gentians, with deep blue-violet flowers

Fig. 11 G. *asclepiadea*

79

produced in abundance over a long period (September/October) on erect stems. 'Closed gentians', in which the corolla remains tightly sealed like a bud, would seem unlikely to get fertilised. Not a bit of it: bumble bees force their way in.

Propagation is by seed. The plant grows well in an acid soil with organic matter and a reasonable amount of sun.

Gentiana autumnalis L. (N. America)

This is probably one of the loveliest eastern North American species and it is native to the Atlantic coastal plain from central New Jersey to southern Delaware and from south-east Virginia to South Carolina. Often reaching a height of 45 cm. it produces single flowers on a stem from September to November, usually blue although white and rose forms have been recorded. The leaves are linear to oblanceolate. Its habitat is open pinewoods of the coastal plain with a sandy acid soil which is wet in spring but drains rapidly. In cultivation it needs a moist, sandy, well-drained soil. Propagation is by seed.

G. *autumnalis* is sometimes found in older floras of the region as G. *porphyrio*. Closely related to G. *autumnalis* is G. *pennelliana*, which differs by having petals which are five-nerved for most of their length, while G. *autumnalis* petals have three nerves. G. *pennelliana* is found growing in moist, sandy soil in open sites in west Florida and flowers there from mid–October until late March.

Gentiana bellidifolia Hook (New Zealand)   *Plate 2, p. 20*

New Zealand gentians have certain common features: they are without plicae and they are all white-flowered. G. *bellidifolia* is found in both North and South Islands and is regarded as one of the best New Zealand species. With a rosette of 5–8 cm. across, the leaves are spoon-shaped. The flowering stalk grows to a height of 10–15 cm. with single or multiple creamy-coloured goblet-shaped flowers up to 3 cm. in diameter. There is often fine green veining on the petals. The New Zealand flowering season is from February to March, but when in cultivation in the northern hemisphere, flowering months are June and July.

The species has a stout root stock which exudes yellowish juice if damaged. In the wild older plants produce offsets, which then form a clump, but they do not seem to do this readily in cultivation. Growing naturally among the alpine tussock grass, often in deep hollows where it is protected by the winter snow, when in cultivation it likes a good, deep, lime-free soil, with some peat and a fairly sunny position. Some authorities consider that it needs winter protection.

It is propagated easily from seed, but it is not always easy to obtain this as New Zealand gentians do not produce seed abundantly. For this and other New Zealand gentians Professor Philipson's book *Rock Garden Plants of the Southern Alps* is valuable and informative.

Gentiana cachemirica Decne. (Kashmir)   *Fig. 12*

A Himalayan species native to Kashmir, reaching a height of between 8 and 15 cm. It forms a rosette of leaves which are ovate at the base and in pairs on the stems; the paired leaves on the stems

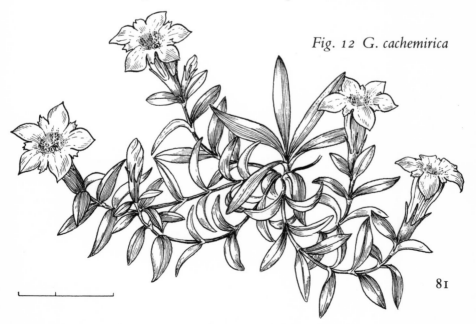

Fig. 12 G. *cachemirica*

81

unite and enclose the stem in a tube. Flowering in July and August the tubular flowers are borne singly, or up to three in number at the ends of stems 10–15 cm. long. This gentian has a clear blue flower with yellowish-white and blue stripes about 1 cm. long on the corolla.

In the wild the plants often grow in crevasses or cracks in the vertical face of rocks, with the flowering stems trailing downwards. Of this gentian in cultivation Wilkie says, 'a position in the scree or in a well-drained pocket in full sun where the shoots can hang over the rock will suit this plant.' It is best increased by seed, which it will set fairly readily in reasonable amounts even in its first season's flowering. It is variable from seed and the examples in cultivation are often linked with G. *loderi*, the difference being the shape of the corolla (more tubular in G. *loderi*), the plicae (erect in G. *loderi*) and the shape of the ovary (stalkless in G. *loderi*).

Gentiana calycosa Griseb. (N. America)   *Fig. 13*

Found in the western states of America from British Columbia to California and east to Alberta and Montana, it grows on rocky alpine slopes and meadows near the tree line. The root system is unusual, being thick, fleshy and many branched, and it sends out shoots 15–30 cm. high. It is sometimes called the 'explorer's gentian' or the 'pleated gentian'. The leaves are ovate to heart-shaped, in pairs, and the bell-shaped flowers borne singly in August/September are a deep purple-blue. As its name suggests, the calyx is large and when in bud the calyx lobes are reflexed to form a star. When the bud opens the corolla is bell-shaped with many cleft plicae.

It is an easily grown species, liking full sun but some shade in the hottest months of the year, a well-drained position and a great deal of water in the summer. In nature it grows in meadows, swamps and on river banks. D. Klaber recommends growing it by the edge of a stream and Musgrave recommended underground watering. G. *calycosa* can be grown from seed or by division in early spring.

Fig. 13 G. *calycosa*

Gentiana clausa Raf. (N. America)

Its distribution is defined by Dr J. S. Pringle as southern Maine and southern Quebec, westwards to north-east Tennessee and north-west North Carolina. *G. clausa* is a large plant which reaches a height of 65 cm. It has glossy green leaves which are ovate to ovate-lanceolate. As its name implies, this is one of the 'closed gentians', its corolla remaining firmly shut, and many regard it as one of the best as its flowers are large. It blooms from mid-August until October, with blue flowers in terminal clusters. A white form is also known. Propagation is by seed. This is a plant which tolerates a moderate amount of shade and requires an adequate supply of moisture in the growing season. It is suited to a woodland garden —it is rather too large for the rock garden.

Gentiana decora Pollard (N. America)   *Fig. 14*

With a distribution from Georgia to Virginia, this gentian grows between 20 and 25 cm. high and has dark green, lance-elliptic to ovate-elliptic leaves.

There are usually single stems with flowers in terminal clusters, appearing in the wild between September and November. The funnel-shaped blooms are predominantly white, with stripes in the blue or violet throat, and it is sometimes therefore called the 'striped gentian'. It enjoys a shady woodland and when it grows in the sun it is usually considerably smaller.

Gentiana farreri Balf. (Tibet)   *Plate 1, p. 10*

'This is the gentian of all gentians . . . the king of the Himalayas.' (G. H. Berry) One wonders what D. H. Lawrence might have written if he had tramped in northern Tibet rather than in the Bavarian Alps, and come upon the gentian that Farrer found and gave his name to. Farrer himself said 'it literally burns in the alpine turf like an electric jewel, an incandescent turquoise.' This little pale blue flower has the quality that makes plantsmen reel, and take gulps of air for strength, it is so pure and so frail. Its trumpet

Fig. 14 G. decora

is the perfect shape to which other gentians must aspire, and it stands erect, head into the sun. First introduced in 1916 it flowered in Edinburgh and took the horticultural world by storm. Pale 'Cambridge' blue with a hint of green, the flower of G. *farreri* has a white throat and purple lines patterning the outside of the corolla.

The plant makes a rosette with many shoots between 10 and 15 cm. long. The leaves are thin, slightly recurved, paired and bright green in colour like grass. The characteristic fine foliage helps to

85

distinguish G. *farreri* from other autumn-flowering Himalayan species. The flowers are usually borne singly on the end of the shoots during August and September.

G. *farreri* likes an open, well-drained position, with plenty of moisture in the growing season—a typical Asiatic gentian, fed by the waters of the Himalayan snows. G. H. Berry, who loved this species, made a special deep pit for it, 60 cm. deep with 15 cm. of crocks at the bottom. By drenching daily the fairly rich soil with which he filled the hole he kept G. *farreri* green and when in bloom, 'a sight for the Gods'.

There is a widespread view that today's G. *farreri* are more anaemic and less interesting than when they excited the gardeners of the earlier part of this century, but there is something about this plant and the cherished possession of it which turns the gentian lover into a connoisseur. It also has the distinction of being parent to many handsome hybrids.

G. *farreri* is not particularly difficult to grow. It sets seeds easily and also can be propagated from cuttings which are struck in late July or early August—at the beginning of the flowering season— or by division in March when the shoots are beginning to appear. It does not divide as readily as, for example, G. *sino-ornata*, but when a particularly good colour form is produced, vegetative propagation is the best way of preserving it. Inferior seedlings should be discarded.

Gentiana gelida Bieb. (Asia Minor)   *Col. plate 11, p. 87*

A native of the Caucasus and Persia, this handsome yellow gentian could have a bright future in cultivation. Though not widely grown it is a near relative of G. *septemfida*, and has the same soil requirements as this easy-to-grow species.

G. *gelida* has no basal rosette, and has stems up to 30 cm. long, semi-erect in habit. The lemon-yellow flowers are borne in clusters at the end of the stems. Leaves are linear-lanceolate, and mainly near the top of the stems. Propagation is from seed.

10 (above) G. pyrenaica
11 (below) G. gelida
overleaf: *12 G. ornata hybrid*

Gentiana gilvostriata Marquand (Upper Burma)   *Fig. 15*

A native of Upper Burma and the Tibetan border, G. *gilvostriata* was collected by Captain Kingdon-Ward and raised in England from seed sent back in 1931. Wilkie describes it as a 'neat and beautiful species, perfectly hardy, presenting no difficulties in cultivation', though others, including G. H. Berry, did not agree with him that it is an easy gentian to grow.

It is very small—only 2–5 cm. high with glaucous green leaves. The shoots bear single, terminal, funnel-shaped flowers during August and September, sea-blue with dark bands outside and purple-blue spots inside. Cultivation is in a well-drained peaty soil in a sunny position. Berry notes that it grew in Scotland in a dry-stone wall given the protection of an overhanging rock. Propagation is by seed or by cuttings from the basal shoots.

Kingdon-Ward really fell for this little plant. He wrote:

> Anxiously I watched G. *gilvostriata*, wondering whether they

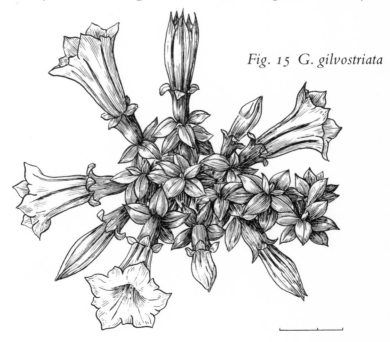

Fig. 15 G. gilvostriata

would ripen any seed before I departed. No insects seemed to visit them nor did the ovaries appear to swell. Every night the trumpets were frozen to the stiffness of thin crinkly paper, every morning they thawed. If the weather remained fine there was every prospect of my gentians seeding even so late as the middle of November.

I was very proud of G. *gilvostriata* when I first saw it in the Seinghku Valley in 1926. It happened to be a very wet year, and before I could get seed of the plant it was buried under snow.

The autumn of 1926 was even worse. I was in the Mishnii Hills and again I found the gentian in flower but not in fruit. Still no seeds. Yet here again was G. *gilvostriata* giving me a fair chance. If I failed this time I would never deserve to see it again. But what a hope I had.

He goes on to say how on this third occasion he found plenty of seed: 'So I was at last able to introduce the lovely gentian to English gardens.'

Gentiana glauca Pallas (Asia, N. America)   *Fig. 16*

This species has a wide distribution, being found from Asia to Siberia and into the Rocky Mountains. It grows 14–15 cm. high with creeping root stocks forming small rosettes of leaves. It is found locally in Japan as a mass of individuals together. The leaves are silvery, glossy green, obovate to spatulate, and single stems arise from the central rosette.

Flowering in the wild is from June to August, and the tubular blue-green (and rarely white) corollas are borne in simple terminal clusters containing one to three blooms. It is a mountain species found at high altitudes in meadows and sandy places. In Japan it is found growing on volcanic ash or in meadows in association with *Saxifraga laciniata*. It is not widely cultivated but it would be worth the effort and would need a well-drained, sandy soil and a cold climate. Dr Gillett notes that 'this species probably could be easily cultivated and would make a fine garden subject'.

Fig. 16 G. *glauca*

An interesting suggestion about G. *glauca*'s taxonomy is made by H. Toyokuni: 'G. *glauca* appears to play an important role in connecting the section Frigida with the section Chondrophylla, because of its similarity to the perennial series species of the latter section.' Its common Japanese name is Yokoyama-rindo.

Fig. 17 G. hexaphylla

Gentiana hexaphylla Maxim. ex-Kusnezow (E. Tibet) *Fig. 17*

A native of Eastern Tibet, G. *hexaphylla* has very characteristic features. Forming no central rosette, it sends up many stems reaching 15 cm. in length. The leaves are small, linear and are arranged in whorls of six, as the name suggests. The lobes of the funnel-shaped corolla are also in sixes, and the flowers are pale blue with six bands and greenish markings on the corolla. Flowering from July to September, its six-fold symmetry should prevent its being confused with other species. A well-drained soil in a sunny position would seem to suit it best, free from lime according to Wilkie, and propagation is from seed, cuttings or division.

Although Farrer introduced this species into cultivation in 1914 in England, and Kingdon-Ward sent home much seed from which many plants were raised, it was a Russian, G. N. Potanin, who first collected the species some thirty years earlier, though his work was largely unpublished as his successor Maximowicz died before he completed work on Potanin's specimens.

94

Gentiana jamesii Hemsley (Japan)

This species has three common Japanese names: Rishiri-rindo, Kumona-rindo and Kawakami-rindo.

Growing between 5 and 12 cm. high, it is a glabrous plant with angled stems, sometimes reddish-purple in colour. The leaves are thick, broadly lanceolate to oblong with whitish margins. The flowers are dark purple with narrow corolla tubes, blooming from July to September. It is raised from seed and best cultivated in a moist, well-drained position away from the full sun.

Gentiana lagodechiana Kusn. (E. Caucasus) *Col. plate 6, p. 69*

Native to the Eastern Caucasus, this species has a prostrate habit without forming a basal rosette. The stems can reach up to 40 cm. but are usually shorter and the leaves are three-nerved and ovate to heart-shaped. It flowers from August to September with deep blue, tubular, funnel-shaped flowers borne singly at the ends of the shoot and also at the axils of the leaves. It is closely related taxonomically to G. *septemfida* but does not produce as much flower, as G. *septemfida* produces its terminal flowers in clusters. G. *lagodechiana* is easily cultivated in ordinary soil with full sun and sufficient moisture. It is readily germinated from seed or cuttings of young shoots taken in the spring.

G. *lagodechiana* was found in the Caucasus by F. Mlokosewitsch (1831–1909), who is also known for the lovely Paeony P. *Mlokose-witschii* which commemorates his name.

Gentiana linearis Froel. (N. America) *Col. plate 7, p. 70*

Widely distributed in eastern North America, with scattered populations as far west as Lake Superior and as far south as Tennessee, this species reaches a height of between 25 and 45 cm. Producing many slender and graceful stems from a central root stock, G. *linearis* has narrow linear leaves arranged in pairs up the stem. Flowering in the wild occurs from July to September, but a little later in cultivation, with violet-blue (or occasionally white), funnel-shaped flowers with corollas only slightly open, borne in clusters in the axils of the topmost leaves.

Called the 'bog gentian' or 'narrow-leaved gentian' in America, it grows in very moist situations often in soils derived from granite. A mixture of acid soils with peat and adequate moisture is best for garden cultivation. Propagation is from seed.

At one time it was confused with the narrow-leaved forms of G. *saponaria* and also the European species G. *pneumonanthe*. G. *linearis* would be a worthwhile acquisition should it become available in seed lists.

Gentiana lutea L. (Europe) *Fig. 18*

Opinions vary about G. *lutea*. Some consider it to be an ugly duckling amongst gentians, though there can be no doubt of its appeal to herbalists, for this is the gentian for distillers. Widely known in Europe as 'yellow gentian', it shares with the annual gentian G. *amarella* the English names Felwort, Bitterwort and Baldmoney, on account of the bitter taste of the extract from its root. Although Culpepper had great faith in it: '. . . a more sure remedy cannot be found to prevent the pestilence', Parkinson in the seventeenth century wrote of it: 'the wonderfull wholsomnesse of gentian cannot bee easily knowne to us, by reason of our dainty tastes refuse to take whereof.' The liqueurs Suze and Enzian are bitter indeed, and modern herbals recommend the use of distilled gentian extract as a tonic. The medicinal properties attributed to the bitter roots are numerous and include cures for gout, fever, chlorosis, foot complaints and digestive troubles, in animals as well as humans. Hardly surprisingly, there is an Austrian saying: 'nothing is so strong as gentian root'. It is the root of this largest of all gentians which is used, and it is a large root, often over 30 cm. in length and up to 5 cm. thick. From this root grow upright hollow stems from one to one and a half metres in height, although rarely exceeding one metre when in cultivation. The leaves are deeply veined and ribbed, paired and joined around the stem. In July and August bright gold and yellow flowers without plicae are

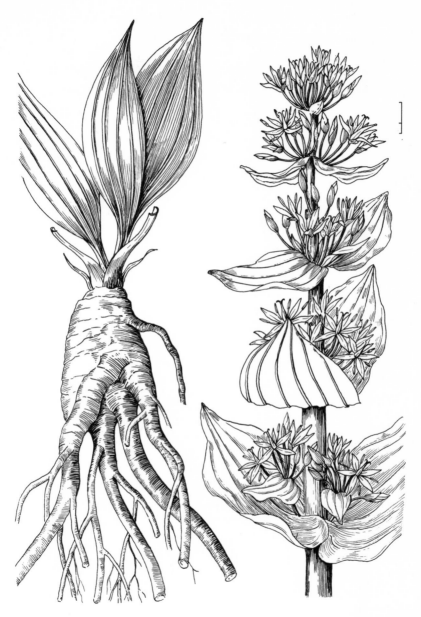

Fig. 18 G. lutea

97

produced in whorls of three to ten at the end of the stem and in the leaf axils. In the wild a brick red form is also known and G. *lutea*, when not in flower, is often confused with *Veratrum album*, both plants being disliked by grazing cattle, and anathema to cowherds, who knock them down wherever they see them.

Moist meadows and mountain slopes form this plant's natural habitat, particularly non-calcareous and unmanured soils. In the garden it grows best in deep, moist, well-drained borders—it is too large for the rock garden. Like other moist meadow plants it requires full sun to thrive. Propagation by seed is best, as the large, deep roots do not divide or transplant well. The species is known to hybridise in the wild and has produced the following:

G. *x charpentieri* Thomas—G. *lutea* x *punctata*

G. *x thomasii* Fil.—G. *lutea* x *purpurea*

Gardening opinions vary about the parent. Wilkie calls it 'the finest of all the yellow flowered gentians', but Berry says it is 'quite out of place amongst the choice gems of the gentian family.'

Gentiana makinoi Kusn. (Japan) *Col. plate 3, p. 51*

Named in honour of D. T. Makino, the Japanese botanist, this is the Japanese species most commonly available from nurserymen. It can grow 20–60 cm. high and the flowers are usually slatey-blue, but variations include white. The upper leaves are lanceolate-ovate and pale green in colour. The leafy stems have several flowers at the tips and in the leaf axils. These flowers have spots on the corolla and are produced during August/September.

It is not a spectacular or showy species, but attractive, with quiet elegance. It is easily cultivated in a lime-free soil away from full sun. The common Japanese names are Oyama-rindo, Kiyama-rindo, and the form *stenophylla* is called Hosobano-oyamarindo.

Gentiana nipponica Maxim (Japan)

A small branching species from the high mountains (around 2,500 metres) of central and northern Japan, G. *nipponica* grows to 5–10 cm. high, with angled stems. The leaves are lanceolate to narrowly oblong-ovate, thick in texture and deep green in colour.

The blue bell-shaped flowers are borne in clusters of three to four, almost without any stalks, at the end of the shoots, and appear in August/September. They are very small, the calyx being only half a centimetre in length. In the wild *G. nipponica* grows in wet and grassy places in the Alpine regions. It can be raised from seed and cultivated in a moist position in a rock garden. Not one of the outstanding Japanese gentians, it is described as a neat little species, but it is hard put to compete for favour with other colourful small gentians. Its common name is Miyama-rindo. There is a *robusta* variety with the common name Iide-rindo. The species is related to *G. jamesii* and the two often overlap in floras.

Gentiana ornata Wall. (Nepal)   *Fig. 19*

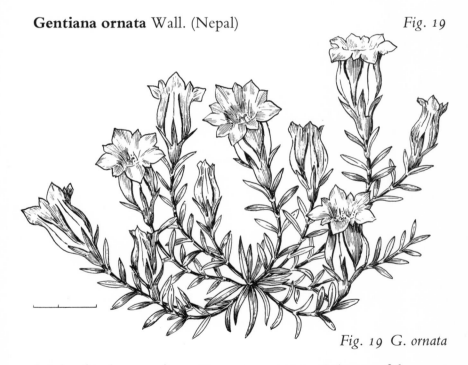

Fig. 19 G. ornata

It is hard to be sure about *G. ornata* any more. It is one of the most beautiful gentians, but the plant has many hybrids, and the

99

original species may no longer be in cultivation. If it is, it is extremely difficult to know if you have got it. In addition, there has been some confusion with the popular flowering G. *sino-ornata*, especially in the early years of this century when the original *ornata* species was barely known. However it is easily distinguished from it when you know what you are looking for.

Originally discovered in Nepal by Wallach in the early nineteenth century, G. *ornata* was not brought into cultivation in England until 1928. It was sent back from Forrest's expedition in 1929 and in 1931 and the plant flowered in Edinburgh in 1930.

It is a neat and compact plant, forming a central rosette from which slender reddish shoots appear. It flowers in August and September and the blue flowers are slightly barrel-shaped, with a white throat and bands of purple, blue and white outside. They are shorter and tubbier in the corolla than those of G. *sino-ornata*, and are borne singly at the end of stems. They have the great advantage of staying open even in dull weather.

Cultivation is in a lime-free soil, in full sun with adequate moisture. Although it may need some winter protection it should not be difficult to grow. It can be raised from seed or carefully divided. The seedlings tend to show some colour variation, and inferior ones should be discarded. The species has been used a great deal in hybridising, which adds to the confusion, but the results are stunning, as can be seen in colour Plate 12 on pages 88–9.

Gentiana platypetala Griseb. (N. America, Alaska)   *Fig. 20*

This species grows in the wild from coastal Alaska to British Columbia. It is a striking plant with mahogany-coloured stems growing from a rhizome and reaching a height of 20–25 cm. The leaves are ovate to elliptical and clasp the stem. The flowers make it unmistakeable: their structure shows a calyx split in two spathes, one bearing two teeth and the other three. Blooming in July and August, it has blue funnel-shaped flowers speckled with green inside. In nature it grows in an area just above the tree-line in Alpine grassy meadows, and an ordinary soil in an open position

Fig. 20 G. platypetala

would suit it in cultivation. Propagation is by seed or by careful division. Commonly called 'the broad-petalled gentian', little attempt has been made to cultivate this handsome species.

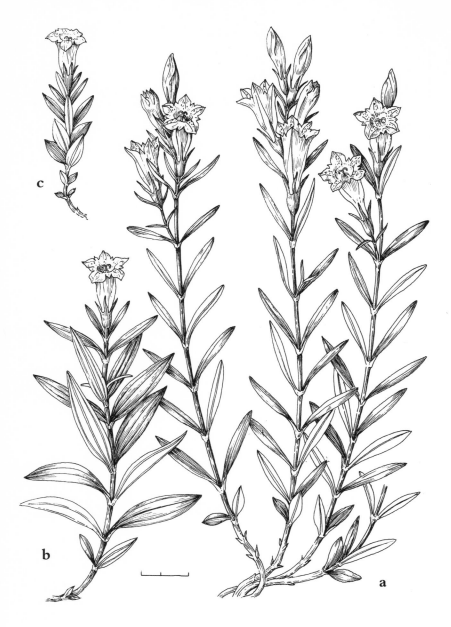

Fig. 21 **a** *: G. pneumonanthe,* **b** *: var. minor,* **c** *: var. latifolia*

Gentiana pneumonanthe L. (Europe, Asia, Caucasus)   *Fig. 21*

This is a British native gentian, often called the 'bog' or 'marsh' gentian, or Calathian Violet. It is a very variable species and forms occur ranging in height from a few centimetres to over 50 cm. Variations also occur in leaf-shape, habit and flower colour. The species forms a rosette, sending up several slender erect stems with linear leaves, slightly recurved, in pairs. The flowers appear in August/September and are deep to purplish-blue, funnel-shaped, with five green spotted bands on the corolla. The flowers are borne on the axils of the leaves and at the top of the stems. Rarely seen in cultivation, it likes a moist peaty soil, with some leaf-mould but no lime. In cultivation it lives for about five years. Propagation is best from seed, and raised from seed it can flower on its second year.

Amongst the many variations the most common, *alba*, is white flowered; *depressa* has prostrate stems about 15–25 cm. long, though older plants seem to be more erect, and 'Styrian form' or 'Styrian Blue' grows up to 15 cm. high with large bells of deep blue. This last form is said to be close to the var. *latifolia*.

In the wild in the British Isles this is a very local plant of damp heaths, and is decreasing, possibly owing to land drainage and afforestation. It is associated and grows closely with *Erica tetralix* and the non-tussocky form of *Molinia caerulea*.

Gentiana puberulenta Pringle (N. America)   *Fig. 22*

A distribution map of this species shows it concentrated in central northern United States, extending northwards into Canada and eastwards to western New York. It is commonly called 'the downy gentian' but the hairs can only be seen at very close quarters. *G. puberulenta* grows about 30 cm. high, with many stems from a slender root stock. The leaves are lanceolate to acute in pairs up the stem. During July to October, the flowers are borne in terminal clusters of one to six; they are vase-shaped and blue in colour, although violet and rose-purple have been recorded. Its habitat in tall grass prairies makes it one of the driest-soil lovers of the eastern

North American species and a light well-drained soil in full sun should suit it. Its propagation is by seed—if you can get it.

Previously known as *G. puberula*, taxonomic work by Dr J. S. Pringle (see Bibliography) has designated the name *puberulenta* to be the correct one.

Gentiana punctata L. (Europe)   *Col. plate 15, p. 108*

This species grows wild in the alpine and southern alpine regions of mid-Europe, the Alps and the Balkans. It is a vigorous plant with a long tap-root from which arise several ridged stems 30–60 cm. high. The leaves are light green and elliptical, somewhat ridged and resembling those of G. *lutea*.

The attractive and unusual flowers, which are yellow spotted with purple, are bell-shaped and stalkless. They are clustered together at the top of the flowering shoots and in the axils of the top pair of leaves, and the corolla usually has a split on one side.

G. *punctata* needs a good depth of soil and full sun in a position where it will not be disturbed. Tolerant of lime in the soil, it is easily cultivated, though still rare. It is a species suited to a large rock garden where it can add height and interest. Propagation is by seed.

G. *punctata* hybridises with G. *purpurea* and produces G. *gaudiniana*.

Gentiana pyrenaica L. (Europe, Asia)   *Col. plate 10, p. 87*

G. *pyrenaica*, as its name implies, is found in the Pyrenees, but is absent from the Alps and reappears in the Carpathians and the Caucasus. Jim Archibald describes this as 'a most difficult gentian' and the species has indeed proved hard to please in cultivation, though he photographed the plant shown in colour on page 87 in the eastern Pyrenees, and its beauty and colour make it a very desirable flower.

It forms tufts only about 7 cm. high with linear glossy green leaves. The striking deep violet-blue starry flowers with yellow

Fig. 22 G. *puberulenta*

stamens are borne singly at the tops of the stems, and last up to three weeks. The corollas give the impression of having ten lobes, but it is the folded plicae which give this appearance. Flowering is in May to June in cultivation and a little later in the wild.

Found in Alpine pastures, usually in turf on damp, acid soil, the most successful method of cultivation seems, nevertheless, to be to treat it as the Himalayan types: to give it an open, well-drained soil with ample moisture, and a position out in the full mid-day sun. Propagation from seed is best, although some suggest division, but as the plant hates disturbance of any kind, I think this method should not be tried. G. H. Berry propagated his from cuttings and found it not difficult to grow, though he could not bring it to flower.

Gentiana rubricaulis Schwein. (N. America)   *Plate 4, p. 37*

Found in North America around the Great Lakes and up to Hudson's Bay, this species is similar to *G. linearis*. *G. rubricaulis* grows about 30–50 cm. high, with red to purple stems and pale green, somewhat succulent leaves which are lanceolate to ovate and obtuse to acute in shape. The long upper internodes make it quite distinctive. The flowers are violet-grey, with attractive forms of white, ivory, pink and blue, and are produced from July to September in terminal clusters of one to fifteen, and sometimes also in the leaf axils. The normal habitat for this species is partial shade and moist calcareous soil, although it is also found in moderately acid soils. The plant associations in the wild include *Thuja occidentalis*, and *Ribes hudsonianum*. A moist sandy soil in partial shade would suit it in the garden. Propagation is by seed.

Often growing near to *G. linearis*, it is interesting that they hardly ever interbreed in the wild.

Gentiana saponaria L. (N. America)

The N. American *G. saponaria* is sometimes regarded as a leafy species, but in the wild it is floriferous and grows to a height of 30–90 cm. The leaves are dark green, linear to broadly elliptical, and between one and seven stems per plant are produced. Arranged in a terminal cluster of between one to eight, the club-shaped flowers of blue, speckled with green inside, are produced over a long period from August to mid-November. The flowers are nearly closed, except in some individuals from the eastern part of its range of distribution which have open corollas. It inhabits moist or seasonally wet thickets, and a moist acid soil in partial shade would suit it in cultivation. Propagation is by seed. This is a wide-ranging species, varying in size, habit and distribution. It is named for its vegetative resemblance to the genus *Saponaria*. Every attempt should be made to grow the better forms and not those which are 'all leaf'.

Gentiana saxosa Forst. (New Zealand)   *Col. plate 13, p. 90*

Confined in the wild to the coastal areas of New Zealand, chiefly on the sandhills of Stewart Island, this is a prostrate species with dark green, glossy, succulent leaves, reaching a height of only 5–7 cm. when in flower. It makes a neat, compact plant with a deep root stock. From this it sends out many branched stems, and when it is happy it will cover quite a large area of ground in a comparatively short time.

Flowering in the northern hemisphere is during August, with pure white flowers, delicately veined, produced in twos and fives along the stem. This beautiful little species is easily cultivated: it likes a well-drained situation in full sun with an ample moisture supply in the growing season. It also seems to tolerate a certain amount of lime. It is most easily raised by seed. Not quite hardy, some winter protection is recommended. Many New Zealand species do not take readily to cultivation, even in New

Zealand, but this is one of the few that rewards care. Berry says of it: 'G. *saxosa* is at its best when acting as a foil to the blue gentians.' It is not long lived in cultivation, and it is best to save and sow seed each year to maintain your stock.

Gentiana scabra Bunge. (North Asia, Japan) *Fig. 23*

This is a species which shows a great variety of types, many being most desirable. Growing 30 cm. high with lanceolate leaves, pale green beneath, *G. scabra* produces terminal flowers, which also appear in the leaf axils in clusters of four or five. The corolla is bell-shaped and deep blue in colour with many variations in its markings. The flowering period is from September to November. The species is best increased by seed and is fairly easily cultivated away from the full sun.

The Japanese variety *buergeri* (Tskushi-rindo) is a better plant having larger, deeper blue flowers which resemble *G. asclepiadea*. Other Japanese forms are *saxatilis* (Kumaeawa-rindo), *procumbens* (Kirishima-rindo, much loved by G. H. Berry), *orientalis* (Sasarin-do or Tonani-rindo) and *stenophylla* (Hosoba-rindo), which resembles *G. pneumonanthe*. There are also known hybrids *G. x brevidens* (*makinoi* x *scabra*), *G.* x '*Iseana*' (*scabra* var. x *sikokiana*).

Gentiana sceptrum Griseb. (N. America) *Fig. 24*

Principally native to the west of North America, British Columbia and California, this plant has a stout root-stock and the stems it produces can grow to over one metre in the wild, but less in cultivation. The leaves in pairs on the stem are lanceolate to linear-lanceolate.

The flowers grow both in the leaf axils and at the top of the stalk. They are deep blue and tubular, produced in July to September. Commonly called 'King's gentian', 'sceptre gentian' or 'swamp gentian', it is closely related to *G. platypetala* and would be an interesting plant for a damp situation in the garden since it is at home in bogs and wet places.

Fig. 23 G. scabra, form Kirishima-rindo

Fig. 24 G. sceptrum

It is regarded as one of the finest American species when in flower, and takes readily to cultivation in Europe. It is easily propagated by seed and can be recommended as a suitable water-side plant best placed out of the full sun.

Gentiana septemfida Pall. (Asia Minor, Persia) *Col. plate 2, p. 34*

When so many of the family are delicate or particular when it comes to cultivation, it is a relief to reach a really growable form. G. *septemfida* is, in the words of Berry, 'the no-trouble gentian . . . it does not mind in the least being soaked with water or having the soil powder dry'.

It is a widely distributed plant, in the alpine and sub-alpine regions of Asia Minor and the Caucasus. It is very variable in colour and habit and this is true both in the wild and under cultivation. The many stems reach up to 45 cm. in height, with ovate leaves in pairs, close together up the stem. It flowers during July and August with a narrow bell-shaped corolla of deep blue and the flowers are in terminal clusters of between one and eight blooms. The plicae are nearly as long as the corolla lobes and are deeply divided, giving rise to the name *septemfida*. Farrer, indicating the ease with which it can be cultivated, called it 'a friend of man'. Originally collected from the Caucasus on Bieberstein's expedition in 1800–05, it was introduced into cultivation by Count A. A. Mussin Puschkin. This species can always be relied upon to produce a mass of flowers annually. It sets prolific amounts of seed which germinate readily. It can also be divided carefully, or thick-stemmed pre-flowering shoots can be taken in May or June for cuttings.

Because it is easy, it must not be overlooked. Its flowers are beautiful, as colour Plate 2 shows. If you have never tried to grow a gentian, you would do well to start with G. *septemfida*.

Several forms of this plant are offered in seedsmen's catalogues, including a form G. *septemfida* '*Doeringiana*', which has dark blue flowers.

Gentiana sikokiana Max. (Japan)

This is a species with slender stems 7–20 cm. high which are angled with leaves in pairs. The leaves are spatulate to ovate and the lower leaves taper to the stalk; they have three nerves and are pale green underneath.

It flowers in October/November, and the blue-spotted, funnel-shaped flowers occur in threes at the top of the stem, and often singly in the axils of the top pair of leaves. This striking species can be propagated by seed and grown in a well-drained sheltered position. In the wild it grows in mountain woodlands. Its common Japanese name is Asama-rindo.

Gentiana sino–ornata Balf. (W. China, Tibet) *Col. plate 4, p. 51*

This species is native to north west Yunnan and the Lichiang range. It is one of the few gentians about which there is a wealth of background information. D. Wilkie described it as 'the finest all-round garden plant that has been introduced in this century. It won an Award of Merit when first exhibited in Britain in 1916, although under the name G. *ornata*. It had been introduced by Forrest after his 1910–11 expedition to the Teng-Yueh area of China. It first flowered from seeds from this expedition at the Royal Botanic Garden, Edinburgh and Ness Gardens in Cheshire in 1912.

Forming a central rosette, the many stems produced reach from 15–20 cm. and root readily at the nodes. The leaves are linear to lanceolate in pairs, clasping the stem. The flowers are borne singly at the ends of the shoots, which turn upwards. The corolla is funnel-shaped, royal blue with deeper bands on the outside, and quite distinct from that of G. *ornata*, which is shorter and fatter. The flowers appear in September and continue on into December, depending on the season, making this the latest gentian in the gardener's calendar.

It is not a difficult gentian to cultivate, requiring a rich lime-free soil with adequate moisture but not full mid-day sun. It is propagated easily from the numerous small rosettes it produces in the growing season and these should be split up in the following spring. It will also propagate from seed or cuttings.

Plant associations can include *Erythronium dens-canis*, or in milder areas, *Fuchsia procumbens*. Some people plant it beneath their roses, and others grow it for cut flowers. It is the only gentian regularly sold in flower markets.

Capt. Kingdon-Ward found G. *sino-ornata* growing side by side with G. *georgei*, which is a beautiful gentian not in cultivation, but he never found any hybrids between the two. There are many recorded variations of G. *sino-ornata*. Forrest noted G. *sino-ornata* var. *gloriosa* which had flowers over 7 cm. long, but this was not introduced. He also noted var. *punctata* growing on sunny slopes in moist, gritty soil. G. *sino-ornata* 'Praecox' is in cultivation, and flowers earlier than G. *sino-ornata*. G. *sino-ornata* 'Brin Form' has a climbing habit, although the flower is identical to the major species. G. *sino-ornata* 'Alba' is less vigorous and needs frequent division and a good feed twice a year with top dressing if it is to flourish.

G. *sino-ornata* is frequently used as a parent plant in hybridising. The following three cultivars are noted. They occurred in 1967 from seed collected from a parent bed of G. *sino-ornata* which had been established for about five years. In 1967 a particularly good set of seed was recorded and the plants were in every visible aspect G. *sino-ornata* and not in contact with other varieties. R. N. C. Lyle observes that the forms are all from natural seed parentage and while so many variations should have been produced is rather a mystery.

G. *sino-ornata* 'Mary Lyle' is a white-flowered form with the faintest touch of blue on the plicae enhancing the whiteness of the flowers. Flowering is in August and September and sometimes well into October. It is the same size as the parent and opens well, unlike some of the white-flowered gentians of other parentage. Growth is good but the plant tends to over-divide itself in the autumn.

G. *sino-ornata* 'Marianne Lyle' is a rich flowered cultivar similar to G. *sino-ornata*, the flower colour being a rich glowing ultramarine, while the end of the corolla tube has a definite flat roll back. Five flowers are borne on each stem and are at their best from September until late autumn. Growth is strong and sturdy and the foliage is a very dark green.

G. *sino-ornata* 'Leslie Delaney' is a Cambridge blue gentian, similar to *G. farreri*. It produces its trumpets from August to September and appears to require a richer soil than its brothers and cousins.

Gentiana triflora Pallas (Siberia, Japan)

This is an elegant plant with slender stems 30–80 cm. tall growing from thick rhizomes. The stems are pale green to reddish brown in colour; the upper leaves are pale green underneath, lanceolate in pairs, each pair at right angles to the next.

   G. triflora flowers in August/September with dark purplish-blue flowers borne in the upper leaf axils and at the top of the stem. It is best propagated from seed and grown in an open position. In Japan this species is widely distributed in the lowlands and mountains. The common Japanese name is Yezo-rindo. There are other Japanese forms, *crassa* (Hama-yezorindo), *montana* (Yezo-oyamarindo and *horomuiensis* (Horomui-rindo). The Japanese variety *G. triflora* var. *japonica* varies from the Asian species in having thicker, shorter leaves, and fewer flowering stems.

Gentiana veitchiorum Hemsl. (Western China)   *Fig. 25*

This is a native of Szechwan in Western China. Like *G. sino-ornata*, this is one of the last gentians to flower, often remaining in bloom until November. Also like *sino-ornata*, it was given an award of merit under the name of *G. ornata* in 1909. It was subsequently renamed after its sponsor Veitch, although it was discovered by Wilson in western China in 1905.

   It is a truly magnificent gentian: 'The open bell and right down the tube is all pure deep blue, looking like velvet, and we fear to touch it lest we crush the pile.' (Berry) The shoots, from a basal rosette, spread to about 10 cm. in length, with blunt, broad, dark green linear to oblong leaves. The single flowers have wide funnel-shaped corollas and stay open in most weathers. Capt. Kingdon-Ward said of it in the wild:

   Gentians so frequently screw up their flowers when it rains

Fig. 25 G. veitchiorum

that it was pleasant to find this one staying open in the worst weather. Some closed flowers which I placed in a tin and kept in the warm hut overnight had opened by morning. Evidently they opened and closed in response to a temperature stimulus and not as a direct response to sunshine and rain.

G. *veitchiorum* is not commonly seen. Berry noted that it was still a rare plant forty years after its introduction. This is perhaps because it is not such a vigorous grower as G. *sino-ornata*. Cultivation is in a good soil, lime free, with adequate moisture and not in the full sun. Propagation is from seed or cuttings and it can be divided in the spring. It has been much used in hybridising and G. '*Stevenagensis*' and G. '*Bernardii*' are two of its progeny.

Gentiana verna L. (Europe to Asia) *Col. plate 14, p. 107*

'Delightful, but often short lived', wrote E. B. Anderson, about *Gentiana verna*, the 'spring gentian', the 'star gentian'. This little beauty is familiar for the sheets of blue it produces on alpine pastures in Switzerland, and the cause of much grief to gardeners who find it to be not an easy subject, requiring patience and care.

Like G. *acaulis*, G. *verna* is used by many as an umbrella name for a group of closely related species, and in the details which follow, five species of the *verna* group in addition to G. *verna* itself are described. They all have the unmistakeable star-shaped flower, although they vary in colour from pale grey-blue to the near violet form shown in colour Plate 14 on page 107.

The G. *verna* group is widely distributed across Europe, from Spain and the Pyrenees through most European countries into Asia Minor and Mongolia. Like G. *pneumonanthe*, it is native to the British Isles, being found in the wild in west Ireland (Co. Clare and Co. Mayo) and in Teesdale—all areas of high rainfall.* These two British habitats provide an appropriate soil, for G. *verna* is a limestone lover, and the sugar-limestone of Teesdale gives it what it needs. The Cow Green reservoir of 1970, absorbing 770 acres of its natural habitat, may significantly reduce numbers of wild plants in this locality.

This gentian is a completely hardy plant, resistant to frost and often, in fact, frozen hard in its natural environment for a lengthy

---

* In British floras *Gentiana verna* is regarded as a relict species, like *Thalictrum alpinum* and *Potentilla fruticosa*.

part of the year. It is often found growing at high altitudes, and sometimes in relatively dry alpine meadows. It grows in association with *Festuca ovina* (a grass), *Bellis perennis* (daisy), *Lotus corniculatus*, *Thymus drucei*, and *Salix retusa*. Opinions vary about its longevity: there are records of plants collected in the wild surviving four years in cultivation. It dislikes root interference of any kind, and in the garden needs a light, open, well-drained soil with plenty of humus. After flowering a light top dressing and gritty compost is beneficial.

When seen *en masse*, G. *verna* makes an intense blue carpet of flowers in spring. Individually, however, the plants are elegant and beautiful and I think they gain by a garden position in which they can easily be seen at close quarters. They are ideal plants for a trough or sink garden.

Seed is the best method of propagation, and most plants set viable seed annually. Germination takes place in spring, and according to Berry, who made many experiments, *only* in the spring whenever it is planted. The seed can either be sown thinly in a pan and pricked off in clumps of four to six seedlings, or a pinch of seed can be sown in the centre of a small pot, thinning seedlings later to one or two strong ones. The seed can be sown on the top of a coarse sand such as silver sand and carefully watered-in, as G. *verna* seed does not appear to like being covered. The seedlings are very small with a very long root and great care must be taken not to damage this when pricking out. Successful seedlings should flower in the spring following germination.

There are many variations in flower colour, flower structure, habit of growth and leaf form. Recorded, though not in cultivation, is a yellow flowering plant from the Caucasus and Persia called G. *oschtenica*, sometimes also referred to as *pontica*. Hybrids may occur in the wild, though no scientific work has been recorded on the subject. The nomenclature which follows is based on *Flora Europaea*, and the interested reader is referred to David Wilkie who gives valuable information on distinguishing the species.

G. verna L. (Central Europe, British Isles)

This is a tufted species, the longest rosette leaves being about twice as long as the stem leaves. These leaves are lanceolate, elliptical or broadly ovate. The flowering stems, which elongate after flowering, reach about 10 cm. in height. The flowering period is between May and August, and the saucer-shaped corolla is azure blue, the tube greenish-blue outside with a white line from each sinus. The calyx teeth are lanceolate, acuminate and winged on the angles. A white form is also offered occasionally in catalogues and found, rarely, in the wild. There are a number of sub-species varying in habit and form, particularly in connection with the wings of the calyx. The plant commonly known as *angulosa* has a characteristically fattened calyx and is now named sub-species *tergestina* (G. Beck) in modern floras.

G. bavarica L. (Mid S. Alps, Carpathians and Apennines) *Fig. 28*

The plant forms a mat of thickly-leaved branched stems, and the leaves are about twice as long as wide, obovate to spatulate, and yellow-green in colour. The plant reaches a height of 5–15 cm. when in flower. The flowers are deep blue, with a paler blue tube, and they are produced during July and August. This is a dainty species, difficult to grow in cultivation, needing a moist position in a scree in full sun. In the wild it grows in damp meadows.

G. brachyphylla Vill. (Alps, Pyrenees, S. Spain) *Plate 8, p. 121*

This species has a neat compact habit, forming a mat only two centimetres high. The rhomboid to suborbicular leaves are glaucous, thick and fleshy. The saucer-shaped flowers are deep blue, clearer than *G. verna* and the tube is greenish-blue outside. Flowers appear in July and August. The slender calyx and corolla tube help to distinguish this species from *G. verna*.

Difficult in cultivation, and found growing at high altitudes, this species is best on a scree and seems to show no preference for soil conditions as it occurs on both limestone and granite in the

Pl. 8 G. brachyphylla alba

wild. There are some sub-species showing slight variations, for example *G. brachyphylla alba*—see Plate above.

G. pumila Jacq. (South-west Alps, eastern Pyrenees)

A beautiful species. The rosette leaves are linear-lanceolate, acute and have one indistinct nerve; the margins are papillose, and sometimes have protuberances. Flowering from May to August this gentian is deep blue and 'starry'. The calyx is angled but not winged and the teeth are linear to lanceolate. Again this is difficult in cultivation and it is rarely seen, but it is well worth trying. A position on a scree would suit it best. It is found in limestone areas on alpine meadows. There are two sub-species showing variations in calyx shape.

G. rostanii Reut (Pyrenees, S.W. and S. Central Alps)   *Fig. 26*

Similar to *G. brachyphylla*, this is an erect-growing species, reaching up to 15 cm. in height. The lower leaves are rather crowded, about four times as long as wide, linear to linear-lanceolate with

121

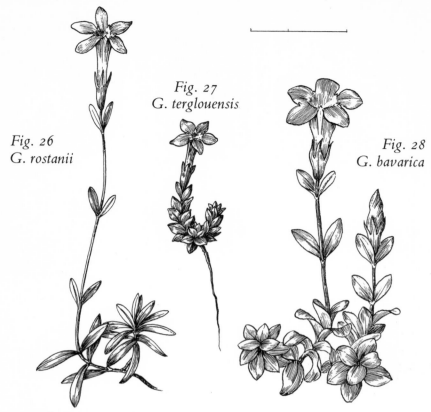

Fig. 26
G. rostanii

Fig. 27
G. terglouensis

Fig. 28
G. bavarica

smooth margins. The leaves on the stem vary from two to four pairs. Flowering from June to July, the flowers are borne on slender stems and are a deep velvety blue. It tends to be rather lank in habit and is rarely seen in cultivation. A position on a scree in full sun is necessary if it is to do well in the garden.

G. terglouensis Jacq. (South and east Alps)   *Fig. 27*

This is a closely tufted species rarely growing over 4 cm. high. The shoots are densely covered with overlapping ovate-lanceolate leaves, as seen in Fig. 27. The margins are strongly papillose. The flowers, which are raised hardly above the leaves, are deep azure blue with paler markings and appear from July to August. Found in limestone areas, this species requires good drainage, full sun and some lime in the soil.

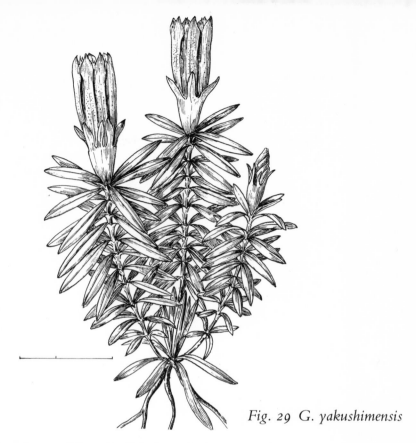

Fig. 29 G. yakushimensis

Gentiana villosa L. (N. America)

This species is distributed throughout the south-eastern part of the United States from Delaware to north Florida.

It produces several stems with dark green, silvery leaves, elliptical or lanceolate to obovate in shape. The flowers, although large, remain closed. They are greenish to yellowish in colour, with green or sometimes violet-blue veins on the outside. The flowering period is unusually late: September to December. Growing naturally in woodlands, a moist damp soil in cultivation should satisfy its needs. Seed should provide the best method of increase. It is possible that the flowers might suffer damage in colder climates (i.e. the farther north it is grown), owing to the lateness of its flowering season, but is worth growing for its foliage.

123

Gentiana yakushimensis Makino (Japan) *Fig. 29*

This is a glabrous plant growing between 7 and 30 cm. high, producing only a few stems from a fleshy rootstock. The leaves are linear-lanceolate, deep green on the upper surface and whitish beneath. The long flowers are produced singly during August and are deep blue in colour. Propagation is by seed and cultivation should be in a moist, well-drained soil, out of the full sun.

Toyokuni describes it as a 'striking plant growing in a very restricted area in the alpine region of the Island of Yaku, with thick long roots penetrating deeply into limestone crevices. Its common name in Japan is Yakushima-rindo.

South American Gentians

No book on *Gentiana* which fails to include the spectacular South American species can hope to give more than a partial view of the gentian family of plants. At the same time the gardener, however hard he tries, is unlikely to obtain seeds or plants of any of these species unless he can travel to the Andes himself, as the two hundred-odd South American species have scarcely been classified, let alone cultivated. In fact, opinions vary among botanists as to whether many of the species should be called *Gentiana* or *Gentianella*. Variety of form is even wider than in the European and Asian species, and many gentian lovers would fail to recognise South American plants as gentians at all. Nevertheless they would hardly pass the plants by as they have spectacular flowers and colours, and for this reason I think it is best to include short descriptions of a dozen or so South American plants to tempt gardeners and encourage botanising travellers.

Since there is very little in common between the plants described, they are all grouped together only for convenience. I am indebted to Dr H. A. Fabris of Argentina and to John Watson, who has travelled widely collecting plants in the Andes, for help and information. J. F. Macbride's *Flora of Peru* (Chicago, 1959), which includes over one hundred gentians, has been invaluable.

17 G. 'Macaulayi'

Sampson Clay, writing in *The Present Day Rock Garden* said, 'The majority of Andean gentians have a corolla which is divided into separate petals for most of its length. Flowers of this type are free to spread out into open cups or shallow saucers and very frequently do so, or they may retain a wide cup or crocus-like form which is equally unfamiliar. A smaller group has more tubular corollas cut into lobes for only half their length or so. Sometimes there is a beard of hair in the throat.' He goes on to note that they vary considerably in form: 'Tiny cushions and quite tall shrubs, solitary sessile flowers or big loose pyramids, or close head-like inflorescences, large soft leaves or minute thick leathery ones.' He also said that the first terminal flower which opens is usually larger than the others. The colours range from lilac and purple to yellow and shades of red, and very rarely do true blue ones occur. 'Frequently a single type, or even a single species, occurs in a whole range of colours.' Some species such as G. *radicata* have the habit of Ericaceae, others resemble Penstemons. One of the reasons why these plants are not introduced into cultivation is that many prove to be monocarpic and seem reluctant to set seed when cultivated.

Peruvian species are probably allied to New Zealand gentians. Many are used for medicinal purposes, and Macbride notes that scarlet-flowered Peruvian species were used by Indians for stock fertility ceremonies called *Pfallchai*.

Gentiana armerioides Griseb.

This species makes a dense cushion 5–6 cm. high and 7–8 cm. across, with many sterile shoots and fleshy spoon-shaped leaves. The flowers, which are solitary, are red or yellow. It is found growing in amongst rocks.

Gentiana cernua H.B.K.

Sampson Clay calls this gentian a 'breath-taking beauty'. The stems reach 15 cm. in height and have big, nodding campanulate flowers, with hairy tufts inside the throat. The flowers are red or purple, sometimes with a yellow tube or lines on the corolla.

Gentiana chrysotaenia Gilg.

Macbride describes it as a showy perennial with yellow striate fiery-red flowers borne on many erect stems, 7–10 cm. tall. It is found growing in stony places and is probably lime tolerant.

Gentiana dilatata Griseb.

This gentian is found growing in moist places, although in a wide variety of localities. It has fleshy foliage and grows up to 10 cm. in height, bearing greenish flowers with violet lobes. It is used as a medicine for ailments of the blood and kidneys.

Gentiana formosissima (Don) Gilg.

A handsome plant growing more than a metre in height. It has a much-branched robust stem with long broadly lanceolate leaves. The flowers—often as many as a hundred at once, and 3–5 cm. in length—are borne on long, nodding flower stems, and are rich crimson to purple or dark rose in colour.

Gentiana gilgiana Reim.

Macbride noted its linear leaves, and large purple flowers resembling those of the families Iridaceae or Cyperaceae.

Gentiana hypericoides Gilg.

A shrubby plant growing 15–40 cm. in height, with shining leathery foliage. The flowers have deeply gashed dark velvety or crimson-red corollas 3–5 cm. long, and Sampson Clay said, 'the effect is unique in the genus'. It is found growing in temperate regions.

Gentiana incurva Hook.   *Col. plate 8, p. 70*

A low, stout-rooted perennial with a rosette of leaves and stems often reaching 10 cm. or more. The flowers are cup-shaped and sulphur-yellow in colour, often with margins of fiery scarlet.

Gentiana regina Gilg.

Weberbauer called this species 'magnificent'. He described the stem, often more than a metre tall, as 'web-like and watery within'. The flowers are lilac in colour and campanulate in shape. In the wild it is found growing on limestone.

Gentiana scarlatina Gilg.

This species was seen in Britain in the 1930's, when introduced by Miss Stafford. Growing 4–7 cm. high with red flowers, it is used in the treatment of respiratory diseases such as pneumonia.

Gentiana scarlatinostriata Gilg.

Sampson Clay calls it a 'pseudo-penstemon'; Macbride describes it as 'a beautiful and distinctive species'. It has several rosettes of fleshy, oblong, lanceolate, acuminate leaves, each producing several stems forming an open pseudo-raceme. The flowers are 'drooping bells of scarlet, internally striped with yellow'.

Gentiana weberbaueri Gilg.

A beautiful, solitary-stemmed perennial, having a thick un-branched root with a dense rosette of linear, fleshy leaves. The stems form a corymb 30–50 cm. tall, with nodding red flowers at the tips. This is a plant that is used for adorning crosses and sacred pictures. Found growing in high screes and on cliffs.

New Guinean Gentians

New Guinea is one of those far-away places about which—most of us anyway—still know very little, but most of us know that it has impressive flora and fauna. I have no experience of New Guinean gentians at first hand, and cannot honestly do more than describe some of the twenty-one species from P. van Royen's Monograph on the subject, published in 1964. In this he says:

The New Guinea gentians are all sun-loving plants of

mountainous to alpine regions from 1,700 to 4,300 metres altitude. They are often found in wet or swampy places although a number has been reported from dry open localities on sandy soil. In most cases these localities are periodically flooded.

If introduced, New Guinean gentians will respond to cultivation, and perhaps in the future one or more of the New Guinea species described below will find their way into nurserymen's lists.

They do have certain common features. Flowers, in the classic gentian manner, are usually bright blue and they are borne singly at the top of the stems. One species, G. *ettingshausenii*, was noted by van Royen to show, in some specimens at least, signs of thigmotaxis—movement towards a touch stimulus (these specimens were growing in relatively open positions).

I hope that the following species notes will prove interesting.

G. cruttwelli H. Smith

This species has purple stems up to 15 cm. high and produces light to deep-blue flowers, dark blue outside, sometimes with a green band.

G. igitti van Royen

A tufted perennial herb growing up to 13 cm. in height, G. *igitti* has pale blue or pale blue-violet flowers with a violet tube. It grows in open grassland on peaty soil.

G. juniperina H. Smith

This species grows up to 13 cm. high, and bears flowers which are dark blue outside, and white inside with dark purple spots. Found growing in open grassland.

G. papuana van Royen

This species forms cushions with stems only up to 5 cm. long. Flowering during August with blue flowers which have a white throat, it grows in the wild in open heath vegetations.

6 Hybrids

There is a certain sort of gardener who does not feel at ease unless he is going to work with a fine paint brush, attempting to produce hybrids by the cross-fertilisation of his plants, a combination of science and surprise. Equally, there are many gardeners who feel there are enough true species anyway, and enough to learn about them, without complicating matters by raising new ones. Those who resolutely turn away from hybrids, or stop reading as soon as they are mentioned, must admit that the gentian family has produced some handsome crosses. Most of the G. *ornata* we see today are hybrids, such as the magnificent gentian shown on pages 88–9.

Cross-pollination simply means placing the pollen of one species on the stigma of a related species. Hybrids occur in the wild between gentian species such as G. *lutea* and its sub-species G. *symphyandra*, G. *purpurea* and G. *punctata*, cross-pollinated by insects, and this leads to some difficulty in identification. Carefully controlled hybridisation is quite a different matter, and to the success with cross-breeding the gentian family so far I must add the view that the potential for gentian hybrids has scarcely been explored. Dr J. S. Pringle has written in a recent paper:

The ability of many highly diverse species of *Gentiana* to hybridise is of interest to evolutionary botanists, since it illustrates the importance of ecologic and geographic isolation in speciation, and the extent to which morphologic divergence may proceed unaccompanied by the development of incompatibility barriers or any obvious changes in karyotypes. Also, because many species of *Gentiana* are highly regarded as ornamentals, infertility amongst species in this genus is of interest to horticulturalists. The possibility of hybridisation amongst numerous diverse species indicates a potential for the development of many new horticultural forms through breeding.

The horticultural potential of the North American species of *Gentiana* does not appear to have been realised. Some of these species, such as G. *autumnalis* and G. *puberulenta*, have extremely attractive flowers; the latter was said by Curtis (1959) to compare favourably with the most highly prized Himalayan species.

Other North American species have rather small, more or less closed corollas, and scarcely compare in ornamental value with the better exotic species, but even these may have much to contribute in such traits as habit, number of flowers and hardiness. Further use of these species in breeding experiments should be of value both to systematic botany and to ornamental horticulture.

Aimless hybridising will only lead to confusion, and to the cultivation of inferior types, and all experiments should have some objective in mind, whether it is to breed a plant with stronger growing qualities, larger flowers, or an extended flowering period. Remember it is not only visible characteristics, but also growth patterns which the hybridiser can affect.

Having chosen an objective, and selected appropriate parents, the transfer of pollen is best carried out on a fine, dry day. Wait until the pollen from the intended male parent plant is abundant and powdery and carry it on a fine sable or camel-hair brush to the stigma of the chosen species. Take careful note of what you have done, with dates and, in particular, details of parents, and what you hope to achieve. Although hybrids often carry some of the character of each parent, unexpected results sometimes happen, and if you have a promising result, it is maddening not to be able to remember how you achieved it. Particularly with late-flowering species, you must look after the seed once you have produced it. Seed pods can rot in the autumn if the corolla's are not carefully cut down the side to avoid moisture collecting in the bottom of the flower. The best time to do this is when the flower is beginning to fade, and thereafter a careful watch must be kept for the ripening seed, and the pod snipped off as soon as its top begins to curl back and the seeds begin to show. See page 42. The seeds should be sown as for other gentians (see pages 44–6).

If you buy hybrids from nurserymen, ensure that you know exactly what you are buying and beware of plants grown from the seeds of hybrids. Some nurserymen offer seedlings grown from hybrids, which is like being offered a dip into the brantub without any assurance that there are any prizes inside: the seed of fertile hybrids often fail to come true, and do not show the characteristics of the hybrid plant.

It is for this reason that hybrid stocks are difficult to sustain, as propagation is by division of plants, and occasionally from cuttings or layering. Hybrid plants should be set in a fairly rich, well-drained soil, lime-free, with peat and leaf mould and with no surface water in winter. An aid to watering can be made by sinking porous drainpipes into the ground at intervals, and filling them to the top with water during dry periods. They will benefit in spring from a top dressing of gritty compost made with a neutral or acid stone. Some hybrid plants are slow to increase, but the clumps gain from division every third or fourth year, and the divided stock should be potted up in fresh compost.

The most favoured parent plants for hybridisation—those which have gained horticultural awards—are the Himalayan species, and they build up their resources during the summer in readiness for the next season. There is always a rosette of leaves when the plants have finished flowering. The flowering shoots and roots die annually, leaving new basal leaves and 'thongs' or roots (the roots of these types are referred to as 'thongs' in catalogues). Each flowering shoot produces a tuft of leaves, which makes little individual plants, easily removed the following spring without damaging the parent plant.

The table in Figure 32 shows how the best-known hybrids have been produced. Where the parentage is shown in the conventional way, e.g. G. 'Devonhall' as G. ornata x G. farreri, the first-named parent is the female or seed-bearing plant. Where the relationship of the plants is reversed, the result is called an opposite cross, thus, G. farreri x G. ornata producing G. 'Farorna' is an opposite cross to G. 'Devonhall', and this particular hybrid won an Award of Merit for G. H. Berry in 1946. Active hybridisation is carried out today by such gentian specialists as Jack Drake, whose 'Alpha' and 'Omega' hybrids I have recently grown for the first time, and Colonel J. H. Stitt, to whom I am indebted for the beautiful photograph on page 126 of his own G. 'Ida K'.

Gentiana 'Alpha' and 'Omega'
Two outstanding hybrids raised at the Jack Drake Nursery at Aviemore, Inverness-shire, of *Hexa-farreri* parentage, they flower in September/October, and both have a corolla of good size and shape, striped on the inside. In 'Alpha' there is a white centre to the throat. Both are vigorous and produce an abundance of flowers. The shoots layer well.

Gentiana 'Apollo'
This has a strong growing habit, having flowers a little deeper in colour than Cambridge blue. The flowers are well turned over, as in G. ornata. It is a cross between G. 'Inverleith' and G. ornata. Raised by H. Bawden of Honiton, Devon, it was exhibited in 1969.

Gentiana 'Bernardii'
This is a strongly-growing hybrid with broad leaves, like its G. veitchiorum parent, growing from a central rosette. The flowers are tubular in shape but there is a pronounced reflex of the corolla and the petals are a deep blue with yellow bands on the outside. Very regular, rather angular flowers are borne singly at the end of each stem, and they come in August. It propagates by division, and it increases well in my garden. It was bred by R. H. Macaulay, who also raised G. 'Macaulayi' and he named this one after his brother

Bernard. Its parentage is stated as being *G. sino-ornata* x *G. veitchiorum* in the Royal Horticultural Society's Dictionary but other authorities quote it as *G. veitchiorum* x *G. sino-ornata*. In 1970 it received an Award of Merit when shown by Dr and Mrs Simson Hall of Edinburgh.

Gentiana 'Caroli' *Fig. 30*

Gentiana 'Caroli' is a rather weakly-growing gentian, but any deficiency in growth is made up for by the charming blue flowers. These are single, star-shaped, striped, pale blue and about 5 cm. long, and they appear in September/October. It is easy to layer, rooting down well along the stem, and it is a hybrid deserving more attention. The parentage is *G. farreri* x *G. lawrencei*.

Gentiana 'Christine Jean'

I have had only one flower this season—my first—but it is a beautiful violet-purple colour with a rich purple sheen on the corolla. It is produced at the end of the stem in September/October and the flowers are medium-sized.

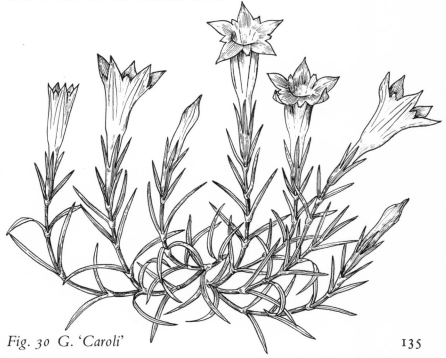

Fig. 30 G. 'Caroli'

135

Gentiana 'Coronation'

This is a floriferous hybrid with flowering stems about 8 cm. long, leafy and prostrate for most of their length but turned up at the tip. Each stem bears a solitary cobalt-blue flower which has green stripes on the outside. The foliage is narrow and grassy like its *G. farreri* parent. N. C. Lyle of Maryfield Nurseries raised the plant in 1953 with *G. farreri* as the seed parent, but the pollen parent is unknown. It received an Award of Merit in 1959 and was described as 'a good free-flowering hybrid'.

Gentiana 'Davidii'

A cross between *G. prolata* and *G. lawrencei*, it has single, pale sky-blue flowers on branched stems about 4 cm. long and flowers in September.

Gentiana 'Devonhall'

A tufted, compact plant with pale blue flowers and paler throat spotted with green, the flowers are 5 cm. long and open in August/September. This is another Himalayan hybrid raised by Mr A. Harley from *G. ornata* x *G. farreri*, and received a First Class Certificate in 1936.

Gentiana 'Drake's Strain'

A late-summer flowering hybrid, the plants are described as having fat dumpy bells of vivid Cambridge blue, usually with a white throat. The plants form thick compact mats. This hybrid is the progeny of *G. ornata* and *G. farreri* from Jack Drake's Nursery in Scotland.

Gentiana 'Edina'

Raised at Edinburgh by crossing *G. ornata* with *G. prolata*, this plant has the habit of *G. ornata* and carries several flowers to the stem, of a darker blue than *G. ornata*.

Gentiana 'Elizabeth Brand'

Similar in appearance to G. 'Inverleith', it has shorter prostrate stems which are mahogany red in colour. The flowers are a kingfisher blue, about 5 cm. long and 3.5 cm. across. The original seedling was found by the head propagator at Col. J. H. Stitt's nursery in Blairgowrie, and named after her. A G. 'Macaulayi' cross, it received a Preliminary Commendation in 1966 when shown by Col. J. H. Stitt.

Gentiana 'Farorna'

One of the late G. H. Berry's hybrids, raised by crossing G. farreri with G. ornata, it received an Award of Merit in 1946. In general appearance nearer to G. ornata than to G. farreri, it has a neat, low growing habit with short flowering stems and flower stalks, with flowers of medium blue, striped outside.

Gentiana 'Fasta Highlands'

This is a vigorous plant with large flowers, varying in colour from pale to deep blue. G. H. Berry raised this hybrid by crossing G. farreri with G. 'Stevenagensis'. ('Highlands' was the name of Mr Berry's home in Enfield.)

Gentiana 'Glendevon'

This fine, free-flowering hybrid has a compact habit with deep-blue flowers borne on short flowering stems. The outside of the tube is coloured purplish, with less light colouring than G. sino-ornata. The parents were G. ornata and G. sino-ornata and it was raised by Mr A. Harley, who gained an Award of Merit for it in 1937.

Gentiana x hascombensis

Two closely allied species, G. lagodechiana x G. septemfida var. cordifolia, were crossed giving a hybrid which produces many large, open blue flowers per head. An Award of Merit was given in 1929 when this hybrid was exhibited by Mr Musgrave.

Gentiana 'Hexa-farreri'

Another very fine hybrid, the flowers being barrel-shaped, six-petalled with long tips, with leaves in whorls of three to five. Under ideal conditions it will flower well in August, and increase rapidly. Its habit is more compact than G. farreri, but stronger in growth and larger in flower than the seed parent G. hexaphylla. 'A remarkable gentian hybrid,' wrote G. H. Berry, 'because it is so much easier to grow than either of its parents.'

Fig. 31
G. *'Hexa-farreri'*

Mr A. G. Weeks of Limbfield raised the plant and it achieved an Award of Merit in 1931.

Gentiana 'Ida K' *Col. plate 19, p. 126*

This was raised from the seed of G. *ornata* sent to Mr Berry from Nepal, who passed some on to Col. J. H. Stitt. Col. Stitt flowered about twenty plants and the most outstanding he named after his wife.

Gentiana 'Inez Weeks'
A G. *'Hexa-farreri'* seedling, it is a strongly-growing hybrid with ten to fourteen flowers to a stem and a paler blue flower than the original hybrid.

Gentiana 'Inshriach Hybrids'
These are seedlings raised at Jack Drake's Nursery, originally from G. *'Kingfisher'*.

Gentiana 'Inverleith'   *Col. plate 18, p. 126*
Although inclined to be of a straggly habit, the outstanding large clear blue flowers make this a desirable garden plant described by Berry as the largest of all gentians. With larger foliage than G. *veitchiorum*, the seed parent, and broader than G. *farreri*, the pollen parent, the flower shape is between the two. It is completely hardy and increases well by division. Mr W. E. MacKenzie of the Royal Botanic Garden, Edinburgh, produced this hybrid in 1938. It was not until 1952 that an Award of Merit was given.

Gentiana 'Kidbrooke Seedling'
This is a strong vigorous form of G. *'Macaulayi'* with larger flowers of a deeper blue. Having G. *sino-ornata* x G. *farreri* as its parents, it received an Award of Merit in 1935.

Gentiana 'Kidora'
Another hybrid exhibited by G. H. Berry in 1952, it was bred from G. *'Kidbrooke Seedling'* and G. *ornata*.

Gentiana 'Kingfisher'
Classified as a form of G. *'Macaulayi'*, it resembles G. *sino-ornata* but has very large flowers and darker foliage. Flowering is in August and September, and propagation is easily achieved by division in the spring.

Gentiana 'Macaulayi'   *Col. plate 17, p. 125*
An easily-grown plant that resembles G. *sino-ornata*, but the flowers are a lighter blue, the calyx lobes longer, and the leaves a darker green, slightly recurved. Easily grown and propagated by

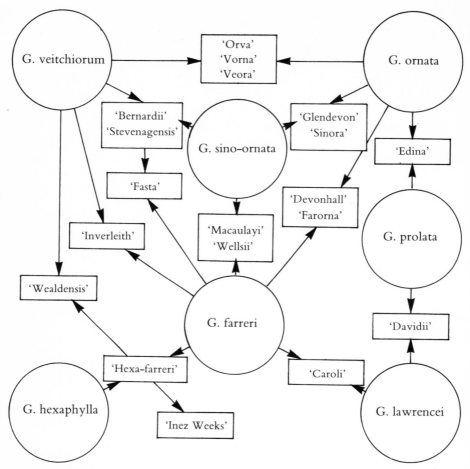

Fig. 32 Hybrid chart, after Chopinet

division, it flowers a little earlier than G. *sino-ornata*, from mid-August to October, and has a neater habit.

This was one of the first gentian hybrids and it received an Award of Merit in 1931. Mr Macaulay bred it in Scotland from G. *sino-ornata* and G. *farreri*.

Gentiana 'Macaulayi Wellsii'

Very similar to the type plant, it has a paler blue flower. This plant is an opposite cross, as will be seen from the chart, and it received an Award on the same day as the hybrid just described.

Gentiana 'Midnight'

An 'Inverleith' seedling raised by Col. Stitt, it forms deep royal blue flowers with no bands or spots.

Gentiana 'Orphylla'

Another of the fine G. H. Berry hybrids, it has neat compact growth, and pale blue flowers with a whitish tube. The corolla has six lobes and the leaves are in whorls of threes, or in pairs like the parent *G. hexaphylla*. The seed parent was *G. ornata*.

Gentiana 'Orva'

This was once regarded as one of the finest garden hybrids. It has a compact habit, and a long flowering period with deep cobalt-blue flowers and dark purple lines on the outside of the reflexed corolla. G. H. Berry raised this hybrid by crossing *G. ornata* with *G. veitchiorum* and gained an Award of Merit for it in 1945.

Gentiana 'Sinora'

This is the opposite cross of G. '*Glendevon*' and it was raised by crossing *G. sino-ornata* x *G. ornata*. It is very similar to the seed

Fig. 33 G. 'Stevenagensis'

parent of the hybrid in flower colour and neat compact growth. G. H. Berry was responsible for producing the hybrid in 1943, but an Award of Merit was not forthcoming until 1958.

Gentiana 'Stevenagensis' *Fig. 33*

This is a prostrate-growing hybrid intermediate in habit between its parents G. *sino-ornata* and G. *veitchiorum*. The flowers are deep purple, lined and spotted greenish-yellow inside and appear in September. It differs from the seed parent G. *sino-ornata* by having branched stems, a narrower corolla tube and deeper colour. Since 1934, when it received an Award of Merit, it has proved itself very satisfactory in cultivation. F. Barker of Stevenage was the raiser.

Gentiana 'Susan Jane'

Regarded as a strong grower with trailing flowering shoots, each produces an ultramarine terminal flower with a characteristic white throat. It is one of the earliest hybrid gentians to flower. It is a recent hybrid raised at Jack Drake's Nursery, the result of a seedling of G. 'Inverleith', and it received an Award of Merit in 1968.

Gentiana 'Veora'

Raised in 1942 by G. H. Berry by crossing G. *veitchiorum* with G. *ornata*, it has darkish leaves with a long flower stem and deep blue flowers.

Gentiana 'Vorna'

This hybrid has flowers of a distinctive deep Prussian blue rather like G. *acaulis*, 4 cm. across which stay wide open in the rain. The plant forms a wide central rosette of flowering stems 10–12 cm. long, each bearing a terminal flower. Of the same parentage as G. *'Veora'*, it was raised by Dr W. L. Lead of Stockport and received an Award of Merit in 1946.

Gentiana 'Wealdensis'

Similar in habit to G. *sino-ornata*, with large flowers of a rich blue with reflexed corolla lobes, this hybrid was raised by crossing G. *'Hexa-farreri'* with G. *veitchiorum* and received an Award of Merit in 1934, when shown by Mr Weeks.

20 G. bulgarica

7 Gentianellas

There are more than 120 species of gentianella in the northern hemisphere, South America and Australasia, and they are not the subject of this book. However, several of them appear in cultivation, particularly in North America where they are quite popular garden plants. One of North America's best loved wild flowers is *Gentianella detonsa elegans*, chosen in 1926 as a symbol of the Yellowstone National Park.

Many of the gentianellas are annual (four of these annuals are described in the next chapter) or biennial, and these are sometimes difficult to keep in cultivation.

In differentiating gentianellas from gentians, J. M. Gillett says:

> *Gentianella* is more closely related to *Swertia*, *Lomatogonium* and *Halenia* than to *Gentiana*. Two groups can clearly be distinguished on the basis of the position of the nectaries. *Gentiana* have glands at the base of the ovary, *Gentianellas* have glands or spurs borne on the surface of the corolla alternate with the stamens.

Gentiana have plicae but gentianellas do not. The 'fringes' come from a different origin.

Gentianella barbellata Engelm.
This is a perennial species. It has deep blue flowers, grows about 5–15 cm. tall and flowers in August and September. It grows in open coniferous woods in Arizona, Colorado, New Mexico and Wyoming. Mrs D. Klaber notes that 'it has a spicy smell'.

Gentianella crinita Froel. *Col. plate 21, p. 144*

This is an annual species, sometimes biennial or a winter annual. The flowers are pale to deep blue, occasionally white. The distribution is from the Appalachian Mountains and the Great Lakes region westward to the Rocky Mountains in Alberta. It generally prefers alkaline soils, but habitats vary according to the sub-species. One sub-species is the much-loved *Gentianella procera*, the 'fringed gentian' as shown on page 144.

Gentianella crinita flowers from June to late September and is often found growing in association with *Thuja occidentalis*, and the habitats are described as 'cedar glades'.

Gentianella detonsa Rottb.

This is an annual or biennial with pale to dark blue flowers appearing from June to November. The plant is found from North America to Europe, into Asia and Siberia. In North America it stretches from the east to the west coasts. There are many sub-species and therefore many habitats; it normally prefers an alkaline soil in tidal estuaries, mountain meadows and wooded plains.

Cultivation of these gentianellas seems most successful if the seed is sown in early spring in a very light, open compost with some ground chalk.

8 Annuals

Of the numerous members of the gentian family, about half are annual plants. They cannot hold the horticulturalist's interest by comparison with the more glamorous species already described, although some of them are very beautiful. Collecting seed from wild plants is the method by which the enthusiast could bring them into his garden, although I cannot recommend this as always rewarding, and the purpose of this brief chapter is to describe a few of the more interesting and familiar annual gentians and gentian-ellas which are essentially wild flowers.

Gentianella amarella   *Plate 9, p. 149*
Sometimes called 'Felwort', this is occasionally biennial, growing 5–30 cm. tall, with purplish-blue flowers. Known for its curative properties, it is widespread in Europe and usually found in pasture, among short grass and dunes. It is common in the British Isles (noted by Gilbert White on the 'Hanger' at Selborne) and extends across north and central Europe south-east as far as the Ukraine. It is not a very attractive flower. Hybrids have been recorded between *G. amarella* and *G. uliginosa*.

Gentiana bulgarica Velen.   *Col. plate 20, p. 143*
Growing 10–15 cm. high, with flowers up to 2 cm. across, this is indeed an attractive annual. Occasionally known in cultivation, its stunning pink flowers are shown on page 143. A native of Bulgaria, it grows in moist, peaty soil amongst grasses. This species is strongly recommended by Jim Archibald as worthy of cultivation.

Gentianella campestris L.
'The Field Gentian'. This attains a high of 10–30 cm. and has bluish-lilac flowers, or occasionally white ones. It is found growing in acid or neutral soils in meadows, grassland and heaths, and occasionally in bogs. Distribution of this species is from the British Isles through north and central Europe as far as Russia and southwards to Spain. It is similar to *Gentianella amarella* and this species is used in brewing as an alternative to hops.

Gentianella germanica Willd.
This species varies considerably from a low, much-branched plant only 7 cm. high to a tall plant scarcely branched up to 50 cm. high. The flowers are lavender to violet or sometimes white. Preferring chalk grassland and scrub in open habitats, often among tall grasses, it is distributed in west and central Europe from the south of England to the south Alps and east Carpathians.

Gentiana nivalis L.
'The Snow Gentian'. This tiny annual grows only 2–15 cm. in height, with tiny leaves and small brilliant blue flowers up to 1 cm. across, which appear in July to September. It is a native of Britain —or rather of Scotland only—where it is found rarely in Perth and Angus, growing on crags and rocky slopes. Elsewhere in Europe it is found in the mountain ranges of the Pyrenees to Bulgaria. A joy, if you can find it.

Gentianella tenella Rottb.
'The Slender Gentian'. Another tiny plant, this species grows between 3 and 10 cm. tall, with single flowers at the end of each stem, pale blue in colour. Liking damp pasture, grassy screes, river gravel and preferring acid soils as a habitat, this annual is found in Europe as far south as the Sierra Nevada, the southern Alps and the southern Carpathians.

Gentiana utriculosa L.
Growing from 6–25 cm. tall, this annual from central Europe has intense blue flowers up to 2 cm. across, star-shaped with white centres. It is found in mountainous regions in Italy and the Balkans.

Pl. 9 Gentianella amarella

Table of Species

Key to cultural conditions: O: ordinary; FS: full sun; DL: deep loam; M: moisture; LF: lime free; S: scree; WD: well drained; Sh: shade; P: peat; H: as for Himalayan species; L: lime.

Gentiana	Origin	ht. in cm. (approx.)	Flowering months	Colour	Cultural conditions	Illust. on page
acaulis	Europe	5–10	5–6	blue	O, S	52, 62
affinis	N. America	30	8–9	blue	FS, M, LF	74
alba	N. America	60	8–9	white/green	M, LF	27
alpina	Europe	5–10	5–6	blue	O, LF	33
algida	N. America/Asia	5–20	8–9	yellow/green	S	77
altaica	Mongolia	5–8	5–6	blue	S	
amoena	Himalayas	3–8	8–10	white/blue	S	
amplicrater	Tibet	8	9	mauve/blue	WD	
angustifolia	Europe	5–10	7	blue	O	73
andrewsii	N. America	30	8–10	blue/white	M, Sh, P	70
armerioides	S. America	6–8		red/yellow		
asclepiadea	Europe	60	7–8	blue	M	79
austromontana	N. America	20–30	9–10	blue	LF	
autumnalis	N. America	25	9–11	blue	M, WD	
bavarica	Europe	5–15	7–8	blue	M	122
bellidifolia	New Zealand	15	6–7	white	S	20
boryi	Spain	5–8	5–7	blue	M, WD	
brachyphylla	Europe	2–8	5–6	blue	S	121
burseri	Europe	60	7–8	yellow	DL	
cachemirica	Himalayas	15–25	7–8	blue	FS, M, S, WD	81
calycosa	N. America	15–30	7–9	purple/blue	FS, M, WD	83
cephalantha	China	15	9–10	blue	DL	
cerina	New Zealand	10–36	8–9	white	S	
cernua	S. America	15		red		
chrysotaenia	S. America	7–10		red		
clausa	N. America	60	8–9	blue	M, LF	
clusii	Europe	8–10	5–6	blue	O	73
crassicaulis	Yunnan	30–60	7–8	green/white	M	
cruciata	Asia Minor	15–45	7–8	blue	DL	
cruttwelli	Papua	15	7–8	blue	WD	
dahurica	Asia Minor	15	8	blue	FS, WD	
decora	N. America	20–25	9–10	blue	O	85
decumbens	Himalayas	23	8	blue	FS, S	
dendrologii	China	15–36	7	mauve|white	WD	108

Gentiana	Origin	ht. in cm. (approx.)	Flowering months	Colour	Cultural conditions	Illust. on page
depressa	Himalayas	5–8	9–10	blue/green	FS, S	151
detonsa	Yunnan	15–30	9	blue	M, WD	
dilatata	S. America	10		green/violet		
dinarica	Europe	8–10	5–6	blue	O	
elwesii	Sikkim	37	9	blue	S	
farreri	Tibet	10–15	8	blue	S, P, H	10
fetisovii	China	40	8	blue	FS, WD	
formosissima	S. America	100		red/purple		
freyniana	Asia Minor	15–30	8–9	blue	DL	
frigida	Europe	7–12	8	yellowish	S, L	
froelichii	Europe	2	8	blue	S	
gelida	Asia Minor	30	7–8	yellow	FS	87
georgii	Yunnan	10	9–10	bluish	S	
gilgiana	S. America	10–15		purple		
gilvostriata	Burma	2	8–9	blue	S	91
glauca	N. America/Asia	14–15	6–8	blue	S	93
gracilipses	China	25	8	blue	S	
grombezewkii	E. Turkestan	30	8	pale yellow	O	
heptaphylla	Himalayas	12	9	blue	S	
hexaphylla	Tibet	15	7–9	blue	O, LF, P, H	94

Fig. 34 G. depressa

Gentiana	Origin	ht. in cm. (approx.)	Flowering months	Colour	Cultural conditions	Illust. on page
hooperi	Mexico	7–15	3–4	mauve/white		64
hypericoides	S. America	15–40		red		
igitta	New Guinea	13		blue/violet	P	
incurva	S. America	10–12		yellow		70
iseana	Japan	30	7–9	blue	H	
jamesii	Japan	5–12	7–9	blue/purple	M, WD	
juniperina	Papua	13	7–8	blue	M, WD	
kesselringii	E. Turkestan	20	7–8	whitish	FS, S	
kurroo	Kashmir	12–15	8–10	blue	S	
lagodechiana	Caucasus	25–40	8–10	blue	O	69
lawrencei	Siberia	15	7–8	blue	FS, S	
lhassica	Tibet	10	9	violet	M, WD	
ligustica	Europe	10	6–7	blue	O	73
linearis	N. America	30	8–9	blue	M, LF, P	70
loderi	Kashmir	10	7–8	blue	S	
lowndessi	N. India	5–10	8–9	blue	S	
lutea	Europe	150	7–8	yellow	M, WD, FS	97
makinoi	Japan	30	8–9	blue	Sh	51
microdonta	China	60	7–8	blue	M, Sh	
namlaensis	Tibet	15	8	blue	S	
nipponica	Japan	5–10	8	blue	S	
nubigena	Kashmir	8	8	yellow	S	
occidentalis	Europe	10	5–6	blue	O	
olivieri	Asia Minor	23	6–7	blue	FS, S	
ornata	Himalayas	10	8–9	blue	FS, M, LF, H	88–9, 99
pannonica	Europe	45	7–8	purple	DL, LF	
papuana	New Guinea	5	8	blue/white		
patula	New Zealand	15	7–8	white	S	
pennelliana	America	15	10–12	white	M, WD	
phyllocalyx	Himalayas	13	8–9	blue	S	
platypetala	N. America	30	7–8	blue	M, WD	101
pneumonanthe	Europe	30	8	blue	O, M	102
prolata	Sikkim	15	7	blue	FS, M	
przewalski	China	20	7–10	white/yellow	S	
pumila	Europe	5–8	5	blue	S	
puberulenta	N. America	30	7–10	blue/purple	FS, M	105
punctata	Europe	30–60	7–8	yellow	FS, DL	108
purpurea	Europe	60	7–8	reddish	DL, LF	
pyrenaica	Europe	7	5–6	violet/blue	FS, M, WD, H	87
regina	S. America	100		lilac		

Gentiana	Origin	ht. in cm. (approx.)	Flowering months	Colour	Cultural conditions	Illust. on page
rigescens	China	30	10	purple	O	
rostanii	Europe	15	6–7	blue	S	122
rubricaulis	N. America	30–50	7–9	violet/grey	M, P	37
sandiensis	S. America	2–4	12–2	white	H	65
saponaria	N. America	30–90	8–11	blue	M, Sh	
saxosa	New Zealand	5–8	8	white	FS, M, WD	90
scabra	Japan	30	9–11	blue	S	111
scarlatina	S. America	4–7		red		
scarlatino-striata	S. America			scarlet		
sceptrum	N. America	37	7–9	blue	M, Sh	112
septemfida	Asia Minor	15–45	7–9	blue	O	34
serotina	New Zealand	15	8	white	S	
setigera	America	30	8	blue	M, LF, Sh	
setulifolia	Tibet	15	10	blue	Sh	
sikkimensis	Sikkim	15	7–8	blue/white	M, WD	
sikokiana	Japan	7–20	10–11	blue	WD	
sino-ornata	Himalayas	15–20	9–12	blue	LF, H	51
siphonantha	Tibet	30	7–8	blue	S	
speciosa	Himalayas	15	8	mauve	S	
stictantha	Tibet	13	8	purple/white	S	
stragulata	Yunnan	5–8	7–8	blue	FS, S	
straminea	China	23	7–8	yellow	O	
stylophora	Tibet	150	7–8	yellow	DL, WD, M	
szechenyii	Tibet	8	8	blue	S	
terglouensis	Europe	2–5	6–8	blue	FS, WD, L	122
tianschanica	Himalayas	25	8	blue	O	
trichotoma	China	37	6–7	blue	M, WD	
triflora	Siberia	30–80	8–9	purple/blue	O	
trinervis	Japan	13	8	white	FS, P	
tsarongensis	Tibet	5–10	6	violet	S	
tubiflora	Himalayas	2	8–9	blue	S	
veitchiorum	China	13	8–11	blue	H	117
venusta	Himalayas	15	8–9	blue	FS, S	
verna	Europe	5–10	5–8	blue	S	107
villosa	N. America	30	9–12	white/green	WD	
waltonii	Tibet	15	8–9	blue	FS, S	
weberbaueri	S. America	50		scarlet		
wutaiensis	China	15–20	7	blue	WD	
yakushimensis	Japan	7–30	8–9	blue	M, L	123

Classification of Kusnezow and Pringle

Kusnezow

This classification has been included because articles often refer to a certain section without giving specific details. Kusnezow divided *Gentiana* into two sub-genera and nineteen sections; the second sub-genera classifies *Gentianella*.

Sub-Family – Gentianoideae   **Tribe** – Gentianaceae   **Genus** – Gentiana
Sub-Genus – Eugentiana

Sect. I   COELANTHE *G. lutea, G. purpurea* (Europe, Asia Minor)
Sect. II   PNEUMONANTHE *G. andrewsii, G. makinoi, G. pneumonanthe*
          G. asclepiadea (predominantly American)
Sect. III   OTHOPHORA *G. otophora* (endemic in a small area S.W. China and
          parts of S.E. Tibet, N.E. Burma)
Sect. IV   STENOGYNE *G. rhodantha, G. stricta* (China)
Sect. V   FRIGIDA *G. chinensis, G. frigida* (Asia)
Sect. VI   APTERA *G. cruciata, G. decumbens* (Europe, Asia)
Sect. VII   ISOMERIA *G. loderi*
Sect. VIII   CHONDROPHYLLA *G. altaica, G. squarrosa* (Europe, Asia, W. N.
          America)
Sect. IX   THYLACITES *G. acaulis* (Europe)
Sect. X   CYCLOSTIGMA *G. nivalis, G. verna* (Europe, Caucasus, Siberia, Arctic
          regions)

Pringle

This study by Dr. J. S. Pringle was not an attempt to reclassify the genus, but to determine for each widely accepted section the correct name according to the International Code of Botanical Nomenclature, which did not exist in Kusnezow's day. The taxonomic validity of Section Isomeria is rejected herein, and its species are reassigned.

Sect. GENTIANA (= Sect. Coelanthe) *G. lutea,*★ *G. purpurea* (Europe)
Sect. PNEUMONANTHE Gaudin *G. andrewsii, G. makinoi, G. pneumonanthe,*★
    G. septemfida (Europe, Asia, N. America)
Sect. KUDOA (Masamune) Toyokuni (= Sect. Frigida pp. sensu Kusn.) *G.
    yakushimensis,*★ (E. Asia)
Sect. STENOGYNE Franch. *G. primuliflora,*★ *G. rhodantha, G. stricta* (China except
    one in Mexico)
Sect. FRIGIDAE Kusn. (Sect. Isomeria Kusn. pro major parte, and Frigida) *G.
    frigida,*★ *G. sino-ornata* (Europe, Asia, W.N. America)
Sect. CRUCIATA Gaudin (= Sect. Aptera Kusn.) *G. cruciata,*★ *G. decumbens, G.
    macrophylla* (Europe, S. Asia)

★ nomenclatural type species.

Sect. CHONDROPHYLLAE Bunge G. aquatica,★ G. prostrata, G. altaica, G. ettinghausii (Europe, Asia, S.W. Pacific Is., W.N. America, S. America)
Sect. MEGALANTHE Gaudin (= Sect. Thylacites Griseb.) G. acaulis.★
Sect. CALATHIANAE Froel (= Sect. Cyclostigma Griseb.) G. nivalis,★ G. verna (N. Asia, N. North America, Europe)
Sect. OTHOPHORA Kusn. G. otophora★ (Asia)

List of Societies

American Rock Garden Society. Secretary: M. S. Mulloy, 90 Pierpont Road, Waterbury, Conn. 06705, U.S.A.

Societé des Amateurs de Jardins Alpine, 84, Rue de Grenelle, Paris VII, France.

The Alpine Garden Society. Secretary: Mr E. M. Upward, Lye End Link, St John's, Woking, Surrey, England.

The Canterbury Alpine Garden Society, c/o Mrs B. Hannan, 157, Hackthorne Road, Christchurch, 2, New Zealand.

The Royal Horticultural Society, Vincent Square, London, SW1P 2PE, England.

Most of these Societies offer an annual seed list.

Nurseries

Nurseries in the United Kingdom with a special interest in Gentians:

The author would like to state she is in no way connected with the nurseries. They are specialists in Gentians, and for a wider selection, readers are referred to the advertising columns of the Alpine Garden Society's quarterly bulletins.

Jack Drake Hardy Plant Nursery, Inshriach Alpine Plant Nursery, Aviemore, Inverness-shire, Scotland.

R. Kaye, Waithman Nurseries, Silverdale, Nr. Carnforth, Lancs.

R. N. C. Lyle, The Grange Nurseries, Grange Road, Alloa, Scotland.

Lt. Col. J. H. Stitt, Drumcairn Nursery, Blairgowrie, Perthshire, Scotland.

Acknowledgements

For technical and practical assistance, the author would like to thank the following:

The Alpine Garden Society, Woking, Surrey
J. Archibald, Sherborne, Dorset
K. Beckett, Dunmow, Essex
L. Beer, Bangor, N. Wales
Dr M. E. Bradshaw, University of Durham
British Museum (Natural History)
Bowmans Hill Wild Flower Park, Pennsylvania
S. Dalby, Birmingham, England
Professor W. H. Duncan, University of Georgia
R. Elliott, Birmingham, England
Dr H. A. Fabris, Universidad Nacional de la Plata, Argentina
The Folklore Society, London
R. J. Fulcher, Inverewe, Scotland
Dr J. M. Gillett, National Museum of Natural Sciences, Ottawa
Dr D. Henderson, University of Idaho
R. N. C. Lyle, The Grange Nurseries, Alloa, Scotland
R. H. Mole, Wellington, New Zealand
Dr J. S. Pringle, The Royal Botanical Gardens, Ontario
P. Robinson, Fife, Scotland
D. J. T. Rose, Plymouth, Devon
The Royal Horticultural Society, London
Lt. Colonel J. H. Stitt, Blairgowrie, Scotland
Dr S. S. Tillet, Botanico III Ministerio de Agricultura y Cria, Instituto Botanico, Apartado 2156, Caracas, Venezuela
G. L. Tarbox, Georgetown, South Carolina, U.S.A.
Professor T. G. Tutin, University of Leicester, England
T. L. Underhill, Dartington Hall, Devon
R. E. Weaver (Jr), The Arnold Arboretum of Harvard University, Massachusetts
H. W. Wills, Mount Rainier National Park, Longmire, Washington, U.S.A.
Dr R. Wygnanki, Santiago, Chile

Bibliography

Alpine Garden Society, *Bulletins*, Vols. 1–41.

Balfour, B., *Some Late Flowering Gentians*. Edinburgh Botanical Society, 1918.

Berry, G. H., *Gentians in the Garden*. Faber and Faber, 1951.

Chopinet, R., 'Les Gentians', *Revue Horticole* Nos. 2287–95, 1969–70, pp. 1700–5, 1738–45, 1758–61, 1793–99, 1860–3, 1896–7.

Elkington, T. T., 'Gentiana verna', *The Journal of Ecology*, Vol. 51, 1963, pp. 755–67.

Fabris, H. A., 'Sinopsis prelimnar de las Gentianaceas Argentinas'. *Bol. Soc. Argent. Bot.* 4, 1953, pp. 233–59.

—— 'Nuevas especies de Gentianella del Peru', *Bol. Soc. Argent. Bot.* 6, pp. 45–50, 1955.

—— 'El genero Gentianella en Ecuador', *Bol. Soc. Argent. Bot.* 8, 1960, pp. 160–92.

Forrest, G., *Royal Botanical Garden, Edinburgh. Notes*, Vol. 4, 1908, pp. 69–76.

Grisebach, J., *Some Factors Affecting Germination and Growth of Gentians*, Boyce Thomp. Inst. Plant Research, 1937.

Gillett, J., 'A Revision of the N. American Species of Gentianella (Moench)', *Annals of the Missouri Botanical Garden*, 1957, Vol. 44, pp. 199–269.

—— *The Gentians of Canada, Alaska and Greenland*, Research Branch, Canada Dept. of Agric., Ottawa, Publ. 1180, 1963.

Hitchcock, C. L., et al, *Vascular Plants of the Pacific North West*, Vol. 4, University of Washington Press, 1959.

Huxley, T. H., 'The Gentians, Notes and Queries', *Journal Linnean Society*, 1888, Vol. 24, pp. 101–24.

Klaber, D., *Gentians For Your Garden*, Barrow, New York, 1964.

Lindsey, A. A., 'Floral Anatomy in the Gentianaceae', *Am. Jour. Bot.*, 27, pp. 640–52.

Macbride, J. F., *Gentianaceae in the Flora of Peru*, Field Mus. Nat. Hist. Bot. 1959, fol. 13. part V. No. 1, pp. 270–352.

Marquand, C. V. B., *Kew Bulletin*, 1937, pp. 134–80.

Musgrave, C. T., *The Newer Gentians*, Royal Horticultural Society publication, 1947.

Pratt, A., *Flowering Plants, Grasses and Ferns of Great Britain*, Warne, 1899.

Pringle, J. S., 'Gentiana puberulenta sp. Nov., A Known but Unnamed Species of the North American Prairies', *Rhodora* 68, 1966, pp. 209–14.

—— 'Taxonomy of Gentiana, Section Pneumonanthe, in Eastern North America', *Brittonia* 19, 1967, pp. 1–32.

—— 'The Status and Distribution of Gentiana linearis and Gentiana rubricaulis in the Upper Great Lakes Region,' *Michigan Bot.* 7, 1968, pp. 99–112.

—— 'Hybridisation in Gentiana', *Baileya* 18 (2), 1971, pp. 41–51.

Royen, P. van, 'Sertulum Papuanum 10 Gentianaceae.' *Contr. Anthropol. Bot. Geol. Zool. Papuan Region, Bot.* 17, 1964, pp. 369–416.

Rork, C. L., 'Cytological Studies in the Gentianaceae, *Am. Jour. Bot.* 36, 1949, pp. 687–701.

Simmonds, S. P., *Integrated Control of Pests in Town and Garden*, Supplement to the Journal of the Devon Trust for Nature Conservancy, March, 1972.

Smith, H., New Chinese Species of Gentiana, *Kew Bulletin*, No. 3, 1937.

Thompson, P. A., 'Effects of After Ripening and Chilling Treatments on the Germination of Species of Gentiana at Different Temperatures,' 1969, *Journ. Hort. Science*, 44, pp. 343–58.

Toyokuni, H., 'Conspectus Gentianacearum japonicarum, A General View of Gentianaceae indigenous to Japan', *Journ. Fac. Sci. Hokkaido Univ. Bot.* 7, 1963, pp. 137–259.

Tynan, K., and Maitland, F., *The Book of Flowers*, London, Smith Elder, 1909.

Tutin, T. G., 'Gentian Sect. Megalanthe (Gaudin)', *Fragmenta Floristica et Geobotanica Ann.* 16. 1970.

Weiss, F. E., 'On the Germination and Seedlings of Gentian', *R.H.S. Journal*, 58, 1933, pp. 296–300.

Wilkie, D., *Gentians*, Country Life, 1936.

Index

Species which are mentioned *only* in the table on pages 150–3 are not included in the general index.
Numerals in italics refer to figures, numerals in bold type to colour and black and white Plates.

DATE DUE			